Cooking Greek,
Becoming American

Cooking Greek, Becoming American

Forty Years at Seattle's Continental Restaurant

TASO G. LAGOS

McFarland & Company, Inc., Publishers

Jefferson, North Carolina

All photographs are from the family collection.

LIBRARY OF CONGRESS CATALOGUING-IN-PUBLICATION DATA

Names: Lagos, Anastasios George, author.
Title: Cooking Greek, becoming American : forty years
at Seattle's Continental Restaurant / Taso G. Lagos.
Description: Jefferson, North Carolina : McFarland & Company, Inc.,
Publishers, 2022 | Includes index.
Identifiers: LCCN 2021057754 | ISBN 9781476686523 (paperback : acid free paper) ∞
ISBN 9781476645520 (ebook)
Subjects: LCSH: Cooking, Greek. | BISAC: COOKING / Individual
Chefs & Restaurants | HISTORY / United States / State &
Local / Pacific Northwest (OR, WA) | LCGFT: Cookbooks.
Classification: LCC TX723.5.G8 K37 2022 | DDC 641.59495—dc23/eng/20211213
LC record available at https://lccn.loc.gov/2021057754

BRITISH LIBRARY CATALOGUING DATA ARE AVAILABLE

ISBN (print) 978-1-4766-8652-3
ISBN (ebook) 978-1-4766-4552-0

On the cover: The Continental; proprietors Helen and George Lagos.

Printed in the United States of America

*McFarland & Company, Inc., Publishers
Box 611, Jefferson, North Carolina 28640
www.mcfarlandpub.com*

To my parents, brother and sister and
to the many customers and friends of the
Continental who turned place into poetry

Table of Contents

Acknowledgments

It's actually impossible to fully acknowledge the debts owed to make this book possible. Of course, I am deeply grateful first to Natalie Foreman and later to David Alff at McFarland for their belief in this memoir in the first place. There are also my parents, Helen and George Lagos, my brother Demetre Lagos and sister Katerina Lagos-Tsakopoulos to also deeply bow to. There is Doug Campbell of Bulldog News just down the street from the Continental Greek Restaurant and Pastry Shop who should be thanked, if only because he was a constant and unabashed supporter and ultimately a friend.

Yet there are literally hundreds of thousands of customers in the nearly forty years that the Continental existed that also must be thanked, not simply those that walked through our doors, but also the regulars who never stopped coming. There were famous folks, too—basketballer Bill Russell, Gloria Steinem, French film director Luc Besson, and Mary Gates (mother of Microsoft co-founder Bill Gates, Jr.) to name a few—that graced the small space, as did the Conti super-regulars who sat at the family table almost daily and became friends—Russell Valley, Will Sharp, Michael Maruyama, and many others.

We must also acknowledge the Greek village in Euboea that produced my family and where we were born. This may seem strange, but without that grounding in the village life, where the local cafés provided the glue for the community, the Continental would not have become the social institution that it did. I will say more about this in the following chapters.

And then there's the Continental itself. It's strange to treat a simple shop space as if it were a human being, yet that is my approach, not out of some deluded notion of corporations achieving "personhood," an odious concept to me, but rather as a "living" entity that took on a life of its own; that is, it had a birth, a life and a death. When I decided to approach the book as a "biography," after publishing two previous ones, it seemed a natural step to take: to make the place something more than

Acknowledgments

merely four walls, a roof, a kitchen, bathrooms, a tiny office and seating area, but to instead regard it as a regenerative force that left a legacy in the hearts of thousands. It is in that spirit that I must also acknowledge the restaurant as a living member of the local community and one whose loss is still felt today. It is in this spirit that I wrote this book and the same way that the Continental must also be thanked.

I am grateful to the editing work of Brooke Manning; her attention to detail and her outstanding suggestions singularly improved the manuscript. It was her encouragement that convinced me to complete the text as a stand-alone book; originally the memoir was part of a larger historical survey of Greek restaurants in the United States.

To my wife and daughter, who inspired me to continue even when it seemed foolish to do so. This book was not written to boost my academic career, such as it is, but out of a debt I felt to the Continental and its impact on my life, which I only realized in the years that followed its closing. Without Nektaria and Elisabeth there to support me through doubts and insecurities, this book could not have been finished. I am grateful to both. I hope someday that Elisabeth regards this book as my gift to her, so she knows more about her family's life.

Jennifer 8. Lee's *The Fortune Cookie Chronicles* and Lily Cho's *Eating Chinese* inspired me to take my family's Greek American restaurant and turn it into both a narrative (story) and a chronicle (biography) of a business that impacted many lives in the community, most especially my family's. Both books are outstanding examples of emerging chronicles that give voices to immigrants' lives in the hospitality industry. For too long immigrants have remained silent in the literature; it is time for these previously silent voices to be lifted.

Perhaps that is the greatest acknowledgment of all.

Preface

It was not a happy day for my family. For several weeks after my brother announced on the restaurant's Facebook page that we were selling the Continental and that June 30 would be our last day in it, the disbelief, sadness, and anger raged, and we felt overwhelmed. Nothing in our lives prepared us for such a moment; nothing that had ever transpired in our lives could. This was a unique event, a wake that stretched without end and continues even now as I write these words.

It was eternal death.

We simply were not prepared for the effect of the news about the Conti's closing on its legion of regulars and fans. "Institution," "community center," "gathering place," and "third place" were thrown around almost like machine gun patter, and we had no bulletproof vests to defend its closing or the reasons behind it. The expectation was that my brother would seamlessly take over the operation after my aging parents retired, but after thirty-seven years in the operation Demetre had no will to do so. As the peacemaker in the family, he had done his best to keep the place functioning while dealing with my parents, the employees, the sometimes surly customers, and all the other myriad challenges a small eatery faces. He wanted a break from the long hours, the physical demands of the job, the constant cheerfulness, the squabbles that invariably broke out among the employees, the difficulties of keeping a small business afloat and steady. He really was burned out.

Then there was me. The idea crossed my mind several times a week, but I never felt I had the stomach or inner strength needed to keep the place functioning. I had none of my brother's calm maturity, judgment, and steady competence. I had the creative ideas and big dream visions but lacked the actual daily interest to sustain the restaurant. There were days when I felt up to the challenge, and others, when examining myself honestly, I knew it was above my pay grade. I would have to remain an academic and part-time writer; these milieus were safer and closer to my temperament.

Preface

My sister would have easily taken over the operation and done spectacularly with it. There was no finer server in the history of the operation, and no one glided through it with more energy, panache, easy charm, and effortless attention to detail than Katerina. She turned waitressing into performance art with other-worldly efficiency, cheer, and determination. On Sunday mornings, the busiest time of the week, with the two dining areas full and people waiting in line in the lobby, she glided through the tables as if every DNA sequence in her body had evolved for this purpose. People came to eat just to watch her performance. Yet, after graduating from Oxford University with her Doctor of Philosophy degree, she was swooped up by a university in California in a tenure track position (she became a full professor not too long afterward).

There was no one left to take it over.

As soon as word got out about the retirement, throngs of people—many old customers we had not seen for some time—flocked back. It was a reunion of sorts, the kind that brings back laughter but also sadness. Even as we planned the last day—adding an extra serving of staff and cooks in the kitchen—our hearts were unsure of how it would unfold, and, well, how it would all end.

Forty years is a long time to own one operation, least of all a restaurant. Few businesses are as intense, demanding, perilous, risky, and yet satisfying as owning an eatery. My father, when he got the bank loan to buy into a share of the place in 1974, had no experience as a restaurateur. He had mined coal in Greece and was a plumber when we moved to the United States in 1967. I remember well when the opportunity came up to buy 50 percent of the Continental and how he struggled with the decision. It was about a year before the actual takeover from the old partner that he spent many nights and days wrestling with the question of whether to go ahead.

A friend of the family, a young entrepreneur, was visiting one day when my father presented his dilemma to him. In mostly Greek and some English, he explained to the visitor his concerns that he had no background in restaurants and that he might fail and be stuck with a bank loan to pay back. The visitor thought about this for a while and declared it too high a risk and recommended he not go through with the deal. Yet, strangely, my father was unsatisfied by this reply.

In fact, he sunk into a funk about the whole matter. It consumed his life; he could talk about nothing else. I was then a young teenager, so I had little wisdom to share, but I felt for his struggle. I was not there to hear all the conversations he had about the matter, but I was told later that it was my mother who influenced his final decision to go through with buying into the operation. I can only imagine her exact words, but they had something to do with what my mother didn't know about but the rest of us do—namely, the American dream of owning your own business, being your own boss, having others work for you.

Some weeks after my father was told he should avoid the deal, my father decided to become a restaurateur after all. It was confirmed one Sunday after church when we visited the restaurant. It buzzed with people, all tables filled and servers dashing about in a mad frenzy. I peeked in the kitchen in the back, somebody's version of a sardine can. Is this what my father bought into? Even I—young, impressionable, obsessing over girls, and ignorant to the world—was sure we had walked into a disaster.

This was a long way from our village life. We had been in America only a few years by then, but memories of the past were vivid and heart-rending. I missed the village, its lazy unfolding of the seasons and the freedom it gave its children to roam and explore and never feel threatened by anything or anyone. The village was both a collection of many homes but also one home writ large—its backyard was everyone's space, and we kids took advantage of the wind, the hills, the trees, the streets to play our own games and engage our imagination. When we arrived in America that freedom was replaced by a compartmentalization of life—there was home, school, the grocery store, and church. Outside of that, the world was off limits to me.

My father was involved with coal mining with others in the village. We all worked tending to our plots—whether raising our own wheat (which we ground in the village's mill), vegetables, olives (which were made into oil), fruits and nuts as well as a few animals, mostly for milk, but occasionally for slaughter at Easter. Centuries had sustained this way of life, and by the time I was born, it existed in perfect harmony with the surroundings. It was not completely perfect (petty squabbles between neighbors and families being the most poisonous and garbage marring the landscape before regular collections arrived are but two examples), but it was perfect for me. I still did not understand why we had to leave paradise. "You're going to America—you will be rich!" I heard from various relatives, unconvincingly. Why would anyone be dumb enough to leave their home?

Children cheerfully played even during war, which took some time for me to understand (after seeing black and white photos from the

Spanish Civil War in the 1930s with children playing in rubble), but I knew enough to know that while our life could be harsh (no central heating in our house, no indoor plumbing, few household conveniences), it never lacked for cheerfulness and laughter. It was a happy place, even if the village occupants were not always so. Paradise had a darker side. In one of the most egregious examples, I still recall a young girl of seven or eight with red hair. A superstition existed in the village that red hair was a mark of the devil, so the father shaved her head. I never saw her in school again, so it was not clear what happened to her.

Nothing seemed happy about the restaurant. It was not just the cramped space but the pace of the workers that scared me. Human beings don't, and shouldn't, move this fast. My father was not a quick-moving person; no one born in a small rural village ever is. Like everyone, he left the house early in the morning for the climb to the coal mine high above the village and returned fairly late. He worked hard, very hard, but he never worked fast. Now he had to move at a pace that defied the norms of humanity. I knew he had made a mistake being part of this restaurant, and all of us in the family would pay the price. I just wasn't sure how. How long would my father last before he gave up his crazy experiment and went back to fixing plugged toilets at a more reasonable pace? (I went on a few rounds with him in his plumbing days, so I knew what he did; thoughts of filthy, plugged-up toilets occupy my mind to this day.)

I could not have foreseen what would happen next; my young imagination had no capacity to see how the place would change our lives. We had entered a strange place, completely opposite in feel and temperament and work habits than anything we had ever known, but one that came to change us and changed us in profound ways. When I look back upon that time now, sealed as it is in a precious bottle, I recollect it with both fondness and sadness, not because it was bad, but precisely because it changed us forever. How it did so is the purpose of this book.

In offering the tale of one family and one restaurant, I offer something both unique and ordinary. Our tale is shared by hundreds of thousands, if not millions, of other immigrants. It is special to us, but not of us—the similarities to other ethnic restaurateurs are too great to ignore. But as I write the story of our family, I do so from one vantage point; others must speak for themselves. I encourage other ethnic restaurateurs to do so, if only because these voices are not often heard in our culture. As I type these words, the shrill winds of hostility toward immigrants blow across the land. Questions about this nation of immigrants arise, many unpleasant, some even violently so. It seems that the great American dream grinds to a halt for many, and it is for that I must raise my voice. How it is heard, if it is, is not left to me. But this should not take away from its telling.

Greek restaurateurs do not leave behind a record of their experiences, hence a great deal of historical knowledge and cultural activity related to their contribution to the American food industry go to the bin. This is true of other ethnic restaurant owners, which only mutes their participation in the larger public sphere, leaving behind a narrow band of archival material that does not capture the fuller picture or the diversity of ethnic dining.

Still, I feel deeply unqualified to be writing this memoir, since my involvement with the Continental Greek Restaurant and Pastry Shop as it was known for nearly forty-five years was determined but not always consistent. My father, who bought into the place and later was assisted by my mother, brother, and sister, was the nucleus of its operation, long after other members of the family had taken his place. I remained on the periphery, even when I had a regular shift (as a line and prep cook); partly this was due to my youth and partly to my having little desire to remain in the hospitality industry. Movies were my passion and my dream, not making feta cheese omelets and Greek hamburgers.

As often happens in life, I came to write this book by accident. I had been asked to teach a class on food at the University of Washington, and for one assignment I asked my students to interview ethnic restaurant owners on the "Ave" (University Avenue NE) in Seattle's University District. The exercise brought back memories of my family's forty-year ownership of the Conti and made me confront my own emotions about it ever since my father decided to sell the place to a nice Chinese family (as he described them) who converted it into a Hawaiian barbecue joint.

The closing of the restaurant had left an emotional scar, and the class project helped to heal some of the wounds; the interviews also provided perspective for the overwhelming feelings of nostalgia I held for the place. It was then that I knew I had to write this memoir, which required a more distanced and calmer appreciation of the legacy the Conti left to its hundreds, if not thousands, of loyal and, in the end, deeply saddened customers.

In thinking about how to best express my feelings about the place,

Preface

I decided a memoir seemed the best way to share some of the stories that took place there, within the larger context of family-owned Greek restaurants in America. Ours was one of the many Greek operations that have dotted this great land since the late nineteenth century and continue to do so. Our story is hardly unique; the details may differ, but the core narrative remains the same: the art and arc of immigrants joining that great dream known as America.

Introduction

The association of Greeks with restaurants in the popular imagination is not a fluke. Many Greeks opened restaurants in the United States beginning in the late 1800s, and tens of thousands continue to operate. They also owned other businesses—grocery stores, fruit stands, barber shops, movie theaters, coffee houses, etc.—but they are associated with eateries. To understand why restaurants became the go-to business for Greeks, according to stereotype, requires knowledge of the social atmosphere of Greece.

It was during my dissertation research in my Greek village that this awareness first revealed itself to me. I came to understand the diffusion of new communication technology in the village, but from the start, I kept hearing mention of the local café when it came to the introduction of the gramophone, then the radio, telephone, movies, and television. Since my practice was to conduct the interviews when villagers returned from work and were relaxing in the evening and then translate and transcribe them the following morning, I began to wonder if my research was leading me in a new direction than what I had intended.

Soon I began to ask my respondents about the café and its link to communication technology, and it became obvious that most villagers got their first exposure to the gramophone, radio, telephone, etc., from a village café (there were several village cafes operating at the time before depopulation ruined their viability). What was it about the café that made this introduction possible? That required further explanation, and my interviewees provided it: namely, the village café as a vital social unit in the community, not just a coffee house that also offered food, but one that was a community center, mailstop, posting place for new government decrees, and, in general, the glue of the community. That is where celebrations—weddings, baptisms, and even funerals—took place. The village café (*kafeneion* in Greek) was central to the leisure, and in many other respects, social and political life of the community. In my dissertation, I refer to it as "mediating commons."

Introduction

When Greeks landed in the U.S. in greater numbers, beginning in the 1880s until the spigot was turned off in 1924, the local *kafeneion* served as a place to get coffee, snacks and gossip and to even read a Greek newspaper or two, but also where news of employment could be found, the wheels of matrimony were greased, and familiarity provided some comfort and continuity from the past to their new (American) surroundings. As Greek American historian Dan Georgakas notes, "*kafenia* rather than churches served as de facto community living rooms."[1]

The *kafeneion*, however, was male dominated. This was as true in the village as it was in America. I remember well growing up in my village and seeing my father and other men there; rarely did a woman venture inside, unless it was for a special reason (other than community celebrations) or for an emergency. This mindset simply transferred to the new world. Only with the "steady arrival of Greek women" in the twenty-first century did the coffee house lose its grip on the community and was increasingly replaced by the community Orthodox church.

The majority of newcomers from Greece to the U.S. during the so-called Second Wave immigration between 1880 and 1924 were men, reaching as high as 95 percent, according to Georgakas.[2] The overall numbers speak for themselves. In 1880, there were only 500 Greeks in the United States. Then came the explosion: 16,000 arrived in the 1890s alone, and then 167,000 in the first decade of the twentieth century. By the 1940s, there were around 500,000 living in the United States, a singular part of the American landscape. With the majority male and the importance of the *kafeneion* cemented into their routines, it was only natural that many gravitated to the hospitality industry, and since restaurants became more than just a business but an important facet of the community, this insured its continuity. While other types of Greek-owned business went by the wayside, restaurants doggedly remained to provide the necessary psychological, social, and soulful salve to Greek Americans facing a sometimes cruel, nativist culture.

It was also a business that did not require specialized knowledge. Cooking, a common enough activity of all human beings, could easily be transferred into a professional kitchen, and with enough sweat equity, usually in the form of relatives who provided cheap labor, they could make a go of the business. Even during harsh economic times, folks have to eat, perhaps not as well, but eateries were in the unique position to be sustainable businesses. Of course, the gruelingly long hours and hard work and competition often took a toll on their owners, and during the Great Depression in the 1930s, many went out of business. But many survived and in doing so began a tradition that lasts to this day.

There was a darker side to the rise of ethnic restaurants, and it has much to do with how Americans perceived ethnic cuisine. Cooking, cleaning, laundering—all represent "feminine" domestic work. The changeover from the prevalence of taverns and saloons, traditionally male spaces, in the nineteenth century to restaurants that involved cooking, traditionally a feminine activity, associated restaurants (in the same way that it occurred to dry cleaning) with second-class "female" work. Most of the world's cooking, even today, is done by women. Ethnic restaurants simply professionalized this feminine association despite the fact that the cooking in these eateries was usually done by men. As Krishnendu Ray writes, "'food and eating practices ... are traditionally linked with the feminine.'"[3] In professionalizing femininity and adding their own brand of ethnicity, Greek and other restaurants ensured their second-class status in American culture. This lowly status was not accorded to haute cuisine operations, such as those offering continental or French fare, which catered to a higher-class customer base in urban centers like New York and Chicago. Other more acceptable and often more lucrative occupations—law, medicine, education, banking, etc.— were simply not open to immigrants or at least not *easily* open to them. Restaurants became viable and, in many cases, one of the few businesses available for entry to foreigners. This was also true of the earliest motion picture theaters in the country at a time when films were considered third-rate, "low-brow" entertainment.

The darker side does not rest there. There is the matter of *white ethnicity*. By themselves, restaurants offer important lessons about business activity and entrepreneurship in the United States, particularly as the country became more heavily industrialized. Yet business never takes place in a vacuum. Despite the strategies learned in business school, entrepreneurs operate within a given society. The society that immigrants operated in between 1880 and 1924 was one fearful of aliens. In 1910, 14.7 percent of the population of the United States was foreign-born, the highest it has ever been in the nation's history (then and now).[4] In such a heavily racialized environment, ethnic restaurants represented, besides femininity, the professionalization of difference. Yet, because they were closer to Anglo-Americans than African Americans, Native Americans or Asian Americans, Greeks (and Jews and Slavs and Italians, et al.) became almost white or white ethnics. Had

Introduction

African Americans, Native Americans or Asian Americans not existed, Greeks and others could not have taken the mantle of white ethnicity.

As explored in Matthew Frye Jacobson's *Whiteness of a Different Color: European Immigrants and the Alchemy of Race* and Yiorgos Anagnostou's *The Contours of White Ethnicity: Popular Ethnography and the Making of Usable Past in Greek America*, the initial result of white ethnicity was social exclusion and marginalization for many immigrants and communication only via acceptable cultural attributes like food and religious festivals.[5] More weighty topics outside of food and festivals such as religion, intellectual history, and philosophy were not part of the general discussion because discrimination relegated immigrants to certain fields. Can human beings truly have meaningful social exchanges if the core of the discussions is limited to food and festivals?

Greeks, like other white ethnics, struggled to get out of the ghetto of food and festivals and into other pursuits; eventually, descendants of Second Wave immigrants chose different professions than hospitality and today more or less are considered part of mainstream society. The experience left immigrants wondering if there was a litmus test for being American. Each country is entitled to determine what constitutes a national, but in the U.S., the question has been fraught with difficulty simply because it has swelled due to immigrant flows. What constitutes an American in 1800 may not be the same in 1900 or 2000, or, for that matter, in 2100. Today we have a fast-growing Latino population, vastly different from migrant inflows in 1800 or 1900. In theory, what defines an American should remain more or less the same—someone who ascribes to the values, laws, and norms of the country. But because those values, laws, and norms change (think feminism, the civil rights movement, gay pride, etc.), so does the definition. Being an American seems to always be up for negotiation, as new immigrants from different lands enter the United States and enrich it with their own customs, culture, and values.

The American racial hothouse produced, and continues to produce, hierarchies. It may even be considered "natural" in the sense that all great nations and empires to one degree or another establish racial-legal hierarchies. The difference is that none of the others began life as a democratic experiment committed to the idea of equality and sanctity under the law. The specific problem with white ethnicity is that it reifies social castes; once established, they are difficult to erase.

While restaurants provided a relatively accessible opening for immigrants to exercise their entrepreneurial spirit and economic prowess, it also limited their ability to fully be recognized as part of the mainstream fabric. Ethnic restaurants ensured that their ethnicity was perpetuated, along with the feminization of the work itself. Cooks, servers, dishwashers, "busboys," hostesses—all became servants to the growing middle-class at the turn of the twentieth century. The profession no doubt contributed to the assimilation of these immigrants, whose offspring went on to have careers in mainstream professions. This is how my mother went from being an illiterate English speaker to someone who spoke and wrote the language, and, even to a stunning degree, managed the restaurant despite making the fewest day-to-day decisions.

Socio-racial hierarchies were not simply reserved for the nation's ethnic groups but permeated down to restaurants themselves. It's a fact of the twentieth century, as Ray notes in his book, *The Ethnic Restaurateur,* that French, Italian, and Japanese cuisines are considered sophisticated fare, while Mexican, Chinese, and Soul Food are not. Greek food is somewhere in the middle today and rising. What created this culinary hierarchy was the institutionalization of food, namely, the rise of the Culinary Institute of America.

Not only did the CIA masculinize cooking but it also professionalized it with the granting of degrees and the universalizing of certain techniques. The dissemination of "mother sauces" based on French recipes ensured that a certain kind of "white supremacy" in food was promoted.[6] Cooking, long the domain of women in the household, became a profession akin to medicine, dentistry, engineering, and law. And restaurant critics, lists such as the Michelin Guide, and now various food blogs further enhance and police this profession. The chef today stands alongside the doctor, the dentist, and the engineer in professionalization.

This book is not about the rarified and sanctified world of haute cuisine, five-star restaurants, and their professional caste. They have enough voices speaking on their behalf. Instead, this work is about those forgotten women and men, immigrants, who labor in extraordinary effort, but who toil and eventually die in complete silence and anonymity. They are the voiceless, even as they have fed tens of millions of Americans, from the poorest to the richest, and all in between, with food that is tasty, interesting, and usually delicious. One book cannot make up for this tragic silence, but it at least contributes to a growing body of work that captures the contribution Greek and other ethnic restaurants have had on America's eating culture.

It came at a price.

Introduction

I would not know the extent of the price, nor the gift it gave us, for many years afterward. Like all wisdom, it comes in tiny doses; it's imperceptible to the eye. All we knew in those four decades was that we worked dog-like as servants, catering to people we didn't like or who were rude to us. We never set out to become restaurateurs, yet when we became restaurateurs, I never fully appreciated the large role we played in the community (by community, I mean the University District and environs from which most of our customers hailed). I never quite fully valued the friendships that were made and the singular importance that the regulars had on our lives. As extensions of our family, they helped to heal us during difficult times, celebrated with us during festive ones, and reminded us that we all need a village to survive this cantankerous world. Most importantly, they welcomed us into America, not that they ever intentionally set out to do so. But in being our friends, they made us feel part of society and made us feel American, even as we were aliens and struggled to adapt to our new home. This barrier is the most difficult one for immigrants to cross; the feeling that we are outsiders looking through a misty, locked window at the happy natives inside, knowing that we can only peer in and never join.

This process took place outside of history in the sense that it was not recorded at the time or that it mattered to those on the outside. But it mattered to us, and now as we see the events that led to our Americanization in the rear-view mirror, we can see how significant and vital it was. At the time we only saw and felt the grind, the long hours, the brutal physical demands, the excess catering to people who did not deserve an ounce of respect but who we had to serve—all these forces became the price of owning our business and the ones we had to obey if we wanted to keep the place alive as an on-going concern.

We put our customers above ourselves. That is the price we paid to make the place work. It was a truth and a determination that guided all our actions, dreams, hopes, ambitions, desires. What we missed was that underneath was the gift of America that the work blinded us from seeing. It is visible now, from a distance and in reflection, but at the time we simply could not see it. This is not unique to us; it has happened countless times, and even now, it continues to occur. Perhaps this book will open the eyes of those deep into the work at the moment, so that they can take relief, and even appreciate that it is not merely back-breaking labor but also adaptation into the wider culture.

Are there better ways for this adaptation to work? Perhaps, but I cannot speak to them, only to the one I know, except to say that in the

American caste system, perhaps the adaptation process that the eatery provided us may be one of the best if few ways possible for immigrants to become part of the system.

*   *   *

Krishnendu Ray's views, as important as they are, represent one aspect of the multi-faceted rise and sustenance of ethnic eateries in the United States. Ted Merwin's *Pastrami on Rye* offers the ethnic delicatessen as a key feature of Jewish identity, particularly between the first and second world wars. It was a "capacious, well-trodden, metaphorical homeland for the Jewish soul,"[7] so much so that a customer once exclaimed upon walking into a deli, "Ah, I smell Judaism!"[8] But more than merely reflecting the ethnic soul, the deli was also a ticket into mainstream society. "While the kosher delicatessen symbolized ethnic continuity," Merwin explains, "the nonkosher delicatessen symbolized the movement of Jews into the mainstream of American society."[9] For many Americans, Jews were recognized for their distinctive cultural and religious habits, yet food was a safe exploration zone for them to try since it offered unique alternatives to standard American fare. Like the first *kafenia* in America that catered almost exclusively to recent or former Greek immigrants and Greek Americans, but which eventually became eateries that found favor in mainstream culture, the deli was the ajar door through which the immigrant entered American society and eventually achieved a greater social acceptance. It went from "favorite neighborhood institution" to strip-mall popularity.[10]

This safe zone says as much about immigrant acceptance in domestic life as it does about the route from alien to citizen, from "too foreign" to "too American." The significance of this circuitous, uneasy, and often oppressed path in racialized America cannot be overstated; it speaks of barriers, bars set high, and other obstacles that made the immigrant experience so fraught with insecurity, and this does not include the hostility aroused by white supremacist organizations like the Ku Klux Klan or, for much of its history, the Daughters of the American Revolution. Yet these barriers meant that Greek Americans, like other ethnics, relied on their own wits, will, and creations—like the *kafeneion* or restaurant—to buttress their presence in the country and to eventually ease their way into mainstream society. The Conti, and this is one of the lessons drawn reflecting on its life after it closed, provided that segue into American society for my family. This is true now with recent immigrants, like those from Africa and the Caribbean, hence the emergence

of Eritrean, Ethiopian, and Jamaican restaurants. The process continues ad infinitum, but this does not necessarily mean it is healthy for
the body politic. As I explain in the later chapters, the impact on those
that toil in restaurants to gain a measure of respect in society can be
severe. Both my parents worked seven days a week, my mother arriving at three in the morning to prepare the restaurant and leaving twelve
hours later. Her only days off were when the Conti was closed: Thanksgiving, Christmas and New Year's Day. My father arrived at about seven
in the morning and left at about nine at night, all seven days of the week.
My brother's schedule: arrive at noon and go home at around eleven at
night. On their feet, too, most of the time.

Yet, significantly, whether the Jewish deli or the Greek *kafeneion*
and later restaurant, it was an immigrant space, "for better or worse," as
cultural historian Shachar M. Pinsker indicates.[11] "Every minority group
had its own dedicated social space in America," Merwin reminds us, and
for Greeks, at least in the beginning of their migration movement to the
United States, it was the eatery.[12] While giving them gainful employment, the operation also gave them ownership of their place in a way not
possible in the outside culture. Other avenues of employment were simply closed to them or unattainable. But in the restaurant, Greeks were
dominant. My father went from unplugging people's toilets to running
his own business; the shift was not simply professional but psychological. In fact, he suddenly was the boss of more than twenty-five employees. He, along with my mother and brother, dominated the space. What
no one expected, what my family could not see, was this space educated
them into American existence. Drip by drip, we transformed into community members in a way not possible by other means, at least not at the
time. My father had a sixth-grade education, and my mother didn't rise
above the fourth grade, yet both became important figures in the community. Those opportunities are now taking place in Eritrean, Ethiopian,
and Jamaican eateries, even if those behind these operations may not be
aware of it.

Has Greek food remained ethnic? Is there a point where ethnic
food is no longer ethnic? By this I mean, does our society grant mainstream status to its minority cuisines? If so, this indicates acceptance.
Jennifer 8. Lee, in her *Fortune Cookie Chronicles*, argues that "Chinese
food has ceased to be ethnic."[13] "'People consider it ethnic when it's new
to them and they don't understand [it],'" Lee quotes one of her interviewees on the subject, adding "this is no longer the case for an American society raised on beef with broccoli."[14] At the end of our forty-year

reign as Greek restaurateurs, I did not feel we vanquished the ethnic label. We were still Greek. And Greek we remain. At a time of rising nationalism, it seems jejune to suggest Chinese or any other ethnic food has shed its foreign label. After all, the labels of Chinese or Greek or Italian cuisine still apply, and likely will for as long as these foods are in demand. When they cease to be eaten, perhaps they will stop being considered ethnic.

The question of whether ethnic food can remain so obscures this truth that it is not the food that ceases to be ethnic, but the personnel behind the cuisine that are transformed. As I explore in the rest of the book, the Continental was a locus of contestation minority acculturation into majority society as well as an educational incubator for entry into the mainstream. The food remained the same (in Lee's words, ethnic food as "predictable, familiar and readily available"[15]), but the people behind it changed. If any lesson was gained from the four decades running the Conti, this is it, and it came without planning or expectation or even desire. It just happened and by osmosis. The Continental was our college of Americahood.

I do not suggest that this happens with every Greek or, for that matter, ethnic restaurant; it requires an operation to achieve "third place" status, that is, it becomes more than a business but a safe, comfortable middle ground between the private and the public. Or, as Pinsker offers, it became a place that "emphasizes the interplay between subjectivity and objectivity, the abstract and the concrete, the real and the imagined."[16] The Continental may have offered these traits to the community before we took over the operation in 1974 or maybe they spewed from the family's commitment to the place (a Lagos family member was always present during all hours of operation). It's hard to know when and how the Conti became a "third" place, and maybe like our education of Americahood, it happened drip by osmotic drip. Whatever the causes, we became the beneficiaries of this reputation which lives with us to this day.

No one can fully understand the Greek American experience without knowing the important role that restaurant and eateries played in it. Even now, I shudder at the thought of the legacy we inherited as newly minted restaurateurs in 1974 and the history that we passed on to others after we sold the operation in 2013. I was eighteen when I realized that I was like many other Greek Americans: part of a family that owned an eatery. My heart dropped at the thought, feeling the victim of stereotyping. Forty years later, I realized what a privilege it was to be part of that world and how grateful I was for the lessons learned while in it.

15

Introduction

Even now, I feel wistful about the place if only because it had entered my heart and became a formidable part of my existence.

In offering a memoir, I do not include all the events that took place or a biography of the Lagos family. Instead, I reflect on the events that fit the central thesis of this book of the Greek restaurant as an active space of minority acculturation into mainstream American society. I do not discuss business issues or downturns in the economy that proved difficult periods to get through both as a family and as an operation. Nor do I cover the happy or sad moments that painted the place with the broad brushstrokes of humanity. Those I leave for those better able to interpret them. The events that I do share are those that I personally experienced or were seen through my eyes only. I am fully responsible for the observations I make and hold no one else accountable. I hope that this record I leave behind helps make sense of a section of American history that deserves to be chronicled. I hope that my voice brings honor to this history.

Lily Cho touches upon this aspect of history in her more academic work *Eating Chinese: Culture on the Menu in Small Town Canada*. While focusing on Chinese eateries in small town Canada, she presents them as both emblems of a Canadian culture now vanishing but also as elements of a diasporic story that is not often written. As she writes, "it is precisely at the moment when something is declared to be outdated that the investment in the dating of things, their situated-ness in history, reveals itself."[17] By this she means that we are both confronted with a fact that culture may try to sweep away, not out of some callous desire to eliminate its diasporic history, but because it no longer has relevancy in today's reality. "I want to suggest," she tells us, "that these restaurants illuminate both the difficulty of sustaining the presentness of the past in Chinese diaspora and the need to do so." And this is what I try to do with this memoir as well: bring something from the near past that has vanished but which still speaks to those of us that care to listen. Cho's work touches upon the role that women played in these restaurants, an element that I relate in no small terms with the impact my mother had on the operation. While this is not a feminist work per se, I try to not forget that the Conti was not entirely a male space, as much as it might have appeared to outside folks.[18]

CHAPTER ONE

You Can Eat Here

January 1, 1974, was the official start of my father's tenure at the Continental Greek Restaurant. It was a Tuesday. School was closed that day and so were many other businesses, but the Continental was open. I was not there to witness the event, but it was discussed at the dinner table the following days. I would not set foot in the place for a few months, not until my high school sophomore year had ended, and I had been fired from my first official job as a "box boy" (now "courtesy clerk") at a local grocery near home. I was fired because while training to use the forklift at the back of the grocery store, I lost control of it and rammed the giant fork into the owner's just-purchased, brand-new Toyota pick-up truck. I can, to this day, still see the huge metal prongs slice right into the entire front of the truck like a knife to butter. My father took the opportunity to offer me work as his helper at the restaurant that summer. I was happy for the transition, but the work-life balance in the eatery was not the happiest.

Two things happened to make it stringently miserable. My father's partner in the restaurant abruptly quit, and my father was forced to deal with a new one. My father's former partner later bought a failing diner just three stores from ours and set about to remodel it, turn it into a Greek restaurant, and destroy our business. For a while, it seemed like he would succeed. The turmoil at our restaurant, coupled with my dad's inexperience in the business, brought strain and tension to the family. At the time, we lived with my father's brother, the man who sponsored our way to America. My mother was busy raising my younger sister. Life overwhelmed us.

The second thing that wrecked my summer was the intensity of restaurant work. No slouchers in our family; from the time my family set foot in America, all members were expected to work. My brother took over a neighborhood paper route, and I became his assistant. By the time I was eleven I had my own paper route. At the time we moved from a small house to a beautiful sea-front property, from a working-class neighborhood that showered my brother and me with gifts and cards every Christmas to a fairly upscale area, where the only gift I received was a small bag of unsalted peanuts every holiday. No one else bothered. Another time, a dog at another seaside home bit me.

The work at the restaurant was not like anything I had known in my young life. Kitchen ("prep") work was demanding, tense, unrelenting, and maddening. As soon as we were done with one task, we were hit with another. Ten hours we slaved each day, without a day to rest. Let me repeat that—no days off, so Monday to Monday we worked in the heat of the kitchen as the weather outside microwaved its own heat. By the time I emerged at summer's end to start my new school year, I was ghostly pale and felt like a prisoner released from solitary confinement.

School seemed a walk in the park after my induction into restaurant life. And the next summer it would be repeated. Rise early in the morning at six a.m., drive to the Continental with my father, return at nine at night. Rinse and repeat the next day. Ninety times that summer. When I returned to register for my high school senior classes the following summer, my friends didn't recognize me; I looked like a freak, with the crazed look of someone who had not been much in contact with humanity. And it was true; I had turned into a cooking machine devoid of the customary connection to reality. I had become a humanoid. My friends wondered what happened to me and where I had been. I told them. They shook their heads. "You're crazy," one of them offered. And indeed, I felt as if I were.

From the vantage point of today, from the comfortable surroundings of academia, this seems a long distance and receding memory. It's difficult to explain quite how the labor and toil of restaurant life suck the lifeblood of its members. My father clearly exploited me, but in many respects, he had no choice. He needed help, and he could not afford it otherwise. I needed redemption and accepted his offer. Perhaps I had something to prove; perhaps I needed some direction in my life. Yet somehow those two fateful summers working at the restaurant were my introduction into the real world, not the fantasy one that occupied my my mind involving being a filmmaker. More than delivering newspapers to uppity customers and unfriendly dogs, being a prep cook in a busy neighborhood operation was my baptism into the ways of the world— blood, sweat, shouting, and tears. What I had studiously avoided all my life was now thrust upon me with a raised interest rate.

I came cheap. My father paid me a nominal allowance (in cash—I was not on the restaurant's accounts) yet somehow it seemed fair. The biggest expense of a restaurant, like many other small businesses, is labor. At least a quarter of the overall costs of an eatery go to pay staff salaries. The Continental employed over twenty workers, and, granted that many of them made the minimum wage, the salaries were not high. Yet restaurant work, however low-skilled, required many hands— from prepping, to cooking, to serving, to bussing, to cleaning—and the expenses are minimized by bringing in family members to help. If ethnic families like those of Chinese, Mexican, Italian origin, etc., often huddled together in the same eatery, it was not out of generosity, or its opposite, exploitation, but simple reality—it kept the operation afloat. I didn't know this reality at the time, my father did not bother to explain it to me (I might not have completely understood anyway), and in that regard he was wise. He left me to pursue my other dreams. We had an unspoken agreement between us—I helped him during summers and weekends, and he never bothered me with any other demands.

No other member of the family stepped in to help as I did, although in time both my brother and sister would do so, spectacularly. They became stellar employees, with a grace and calmness of spirit that I

Dreary, wet Seattle weather on the outside, but warmth, family cheer, and laughter on the inside. This is what made this "third place" so special.

never had. My brother became the manager, and my sister one of the best servers in the restaurant's history. I was a loser compared to them, even though to my father I was the guinea pig that he tested to see how it would work with family members joining him in the operation. Perhaps it was his way of replicating what he had known in the village, working together to tend our farms as we had done. Only restaurant work is a thousand times more intense and demanding.

There are two separate worlds in any restaurant—the front and back end, each with its own pleasures and pains, each an inextricably separate world. I occupied the back, with my father, and we let others (his new partner, the servers, and occasional hostess) deal with the customers in front. My space was the hot, grimy, greasy, oily, stinky one of the kitchen and the prep area. The restaurant was laid out in an upside-down L shape, with the bottom line representing the dining room and the long stem the rear preparation area. It was an odd shape for an eatery, due to the way it had grown from a simple pastry shop. Originally a rectangular shape when it first opened in 1968 by two Greek partners, it added the dining area a few years later and became a full-fledged restaurant when the stationery store adjacent closed, and the Conti took over the space. The small rectangle became an L.

In doing so, it created bottlenecks and inefficiencies, revealing the hurried tenor to the takeover. Rather than carefully considering the flow between kitchen and dining area, the two partners created a kitchen without any regard for how the staff would move between it and the server area in the front. It's as if someone had designed two adjacent rooms with only one tiny door in between them, making moving back and forth almost impossible and often ludicrously chaotic. In that sense, the place was more suited to a Charlie Chaplin silent comedy than to the hundreds of customers we catered to every day. On the weekends, the two very busiest days of the week, the ludicrous became insane; we counted the number of times people bumped into each other every day, but after a while it ceased being humorous. It was not merely that the cooks in the kitchen had to navigate a tiny space to produce the hundreds of breakfast, lunch, and dinner plates every day, double or triple on the weekend, but also having to negotiate the traffic of dishwashers, prep cooks, suppliers, and others constantly moving between the kitchen and the dining area.

My father was not an architect, but he knew enough to realize this setup needed serious amendment, and immediately. Or we could simply watch employees smash full plates into one another and, after a while, simply quit in frustration. Worse, the restaurant would eventually lose out to the competition and end up shuttering. I always wondered how my father came up with this idea, or if he borrowed it from others. Or was it simply the peculiarity of owning your own small business that forces management to be creative and single-handedly solve its problems? It mattered not one whit that my father knew nothing about design or altering a space, yet he knew enough to propose a change. The actual cooking area would have to be enlarged, and the space allowed to the traffic to flow around it, without impeding the grill area.

It was an important new step because the kitchen is the heart of the restaurant. Good food can live with bad service, but bad food cannot survive even with good service. In some cases, owners go out of their way to offer bad, surly service with excellent food because some appreciators of ethnic cuisine found this thrilling. The worse the service and the better the food, the more enticing it was to frequent a restaurant. My father never thought in those terms; he wanted to have both a good kitchen and a good serving staff. He took pride in what he produced and thought of the entire experience—from ordering to eating—as having to provide good value to keep his customers coming back.

Even as he never had restaurant experience before stepping into the Conti, my father had an intuitive sense of how things should operate. When his partner left after six months, it was probably because his idea came into conflict with his partner's. Each had a different vision of where the restaurant should go and how it should develop. The partner, originally brought into the pastry shop, had more of an affinity for sweets than cooked meals. The restaurant was an added feature to the pastry shop, whereas my father saw the restaurant as the main draw. They quarreled, and in the end the partner decided to start his own place. My father agreed. What he did not expect, and could not have known (non-compete agreements were not on his radar), was that the partner would open up another Greek eatery to compete directly with him.

Cakes were made when my father became a partner. I remember taking orders for birthday cakes when I began my "summer internship." It was ludicrous, of course, since the Conti was known as a Greek place, but this is what my father had bought into, and he had to carry on the tradition. Not long after the partner left, the cake business ended. Only those recognized Greek pastries—baklava, galaktoboureko, kourabiethes, and some French types like éclairs and napoleons—were kept. For several months we kept getting cake orders, but we simply recommended another bakery, and soon those stopped.

Cooking Greek, Becoming American

I was too young to think about the business implications of my father's decision on cutting down on pastries. We had a full-time baker working for us, and this continued despite the cakes being eliminated, partly because pastries were an attraction and profitable. Also, I think, the staff enjoyed eating them. So, in the end, it was decided to keep them, which, as it turns out, was a wise decision.

In a strange sense, as the outsider, my father came in time to resemble a reformer. Not all his decisions were sound or productive, but he had ideas. Perhaps his outsider status meant he was not tied to ideology and could see matters with fresh eyes. I, on the other hand, just observed and did my job as best as I could. But it was exhausting—day after toiling day, laboring to make lentil soup, avgolemono (egg lemon rice soup), dolmathes (stuffed grape leaves), rice pilaf, souvlaki, and the rest, I saw my youth vanish with little regard or time spent on my most important interest: making movies and trying to get close to girls. I succeeded in neither.

With the nation's bicentennial arriving, which happened to coincide with my high school graduation, it seemed a good time to mark my own move to independence. By this point, my older brother had started to work at the restaurant, coming in to help my father manage it. I asked for the summer off to fly to Greece. I would go back to the family home, occupied by my grandmother, to ponder my future. Already I knew that restaurant work was not my ideal and not the career path I wanted. Glamor was, for me, at least, less toil than what I experienced and could expect at the Conti.

I spent the summer in Greece in 1976, trying to make sense of the restaurant that was now increasingly part of the family's life and how my ambitions would possibly fit in. It was not an easy summer. I had hoped to also do some dating while there, but this proved futile and, at times, even comical. Sensing where I spent most of my psychological energy, one evening my grandmother handed me a wad of Greek drachmas and calmly suggested I go to the nearby town and have a good time. At first, I assumed she meant that I go to a café or see a movie. Then it dawned on me what she had in mind. I didn't take her money, but I did go into town for an uneventful evening.

If the summer was meant for me to have clarity about the course of my life, I returned with little of it. That autumn was the start of my college career at the University of Washington. High school was left behind for the huge campus of 35,000 students. My first class, Psych 101, was in a huge, theater-like room. At first, I thought I was in the wrong building, but after asking other students I realized this was the right location. I never had had a class with 700 students before. The professor, Dr. Keating, in his first lecture recalled as a grad student in psychology he studied abnormal behavior and after a while he himself was exhibiting forms of abnormality. So, what is psychology? he asked. And how do we separate the normal from the abnormal? I had never received such questions in high school, and it revealed to me the wonders of the university. Before the lecture, I was sitting on a lawn, with my new penny loafers (at a time when being preppy was cool), wondering what I was about to step into. After the lecture, I had my answer. It was the world of the mind, exploration, thinking, questioning, reflection. A world, I might add, completely opposite to the one just about a mile away, at the Conti.

When I returned to the United States after my trip to the Greek village, my father asked me to cook on the busiest shifts of the week: Saturday and Sunday mornings. I was to work with another cook, Carol, who became a dominant force in my life. Like other women I have known, notably my grandmother, she was made of steel and honey at the same time. No task was too small and no physical demand too arduous. Yet, the sweetness that erupted at times belied her steeliness and made her more than approachable—she was almost angelic. We worked together for about two years before she decided to retire.

In his book *The Ethnic Restaurateur*, Ray cites a resident of Napoleonville, Louisiana, who wrote to this brother in Italy, "'In America, the bread is soft, but life is hard.'"[1] The demands made on me and Carol were enormous, and physically hard. It's a reminder that whatever technological progress society has made automating some physically demanding jobs, restaurant cooking is not one of them. Not only were we expected to remain standing on our feet for eight hours with no time for a break, but also to handle wave after wave of orders from hungry customers who expected their food to be good, but fast. And the toll is not just on the body but on the mind, too—by coordinating a myriad of tasks that, if not done right, brings chaos and ruin to the meals. We served a variety of omelets with toast and Greek fries (round potatoes with salt, pepper, and what made it Greek—oregano). We always kept a steady supply of toasted bread and deep-fried potatoes stocked. We were drummers who kept the bass drumbeat going while working the snare drum and cymbals at the same time—for eight hours on both weekend days. If for some reason the bread was not toasted, or if the toaster broke (usually during our busy shifts, not when business was slow), or if we ran out of bread suddenly (it happened on occasion), or if the deep fryer broke, or was too hot, or the fries were not properly defrosted, or if we ran out of omelet mix (prepared ahead of time), or the grill did not work properly (the temperature askew)—if any of this happened our rhythm was destroyed and the flow ruined. The ordered dishes would not leave the kitchen, orders would backlog, and we faced a herculean task of restoring order to the kitchen. For eight hours. All the while, we stood over a hot grill, with greasy steam that waffled up to our faces and bored deep into our skin, and crackling, hot oil that bounced onto our hands and arms, but that we had to ignore so as to not upset our workflow.

Winter or summer, the work was the same, the demands on us the same, the hard work the same, and with the expectations that customers would get their food on time without egg shells in their omelet, burnt toast, greasy, uncooked fries, and the ingredients inside the omelet were (a) the correct ones ordered, (b) cooked properly, and (c) did not have any hair or strange objects in them. Hundreds of times per day, and over the course of a year, tens of thousands. Speed, efficiency, rhythm, balance, planning—all these played a role, while Carol and I worked like guards of a basketball team that operated in sync. We knew each other well. We each had our assigned roles and played them to perfection. But all it took was one snafu to stop the operation. When that happened, hell dropped into our midst, and we had to exert massive effort to catch up. Meanwhile, the tickets (the orders) kept coming and coming, and we stared at more than a dozen orders that had to be filled. Hungry customers were not amenable to excuses if their food was late, or ill-prepared. And we did this for hours upon hours without a break and no time to catch our breath. At the end of each shift, I felt as if I had climbed a tall mountain, reached the top, but was too weak to come down. And so it was, each and every day I labored in that kitchen.

Athletes exert their energy and artistry for about three hours; yet, here we were doing so for eight to ten hours, and we repeated it the next day, Sunday. And the wages we received were meager compared to what we produced—a product that was entirely handmade to order, one plate at a time. We were machines. And we were proud.

Why was I chosen for this role and not my brother? It was never explained to me, but it seems that my father needed my brother to help manage the restaurant, something I was too young to do. There was likely no other reason, although it did feel exploitative on my part. He had the more appealing role, he interacted with customers, while I had to remain hidden in a noisy, greasy, hot, and never-dull kitchen. I did not know it at the time, human nature being what it is, but I came to resent his status and detest mine. I felt capable and deserving of greater roles in life than making Greek omelets (with feta cheese) the rest of my life.

At the same time, I was also on the payroll and could pay for my college education. It put me in the position to finance my life, even as I came to resent the loss of my weekends, and with it, the ability to socialize. I wanted to seek better fruits in life than being a line cook in a diner-like operation. I did not appreciate the decency of the job and how it could have led me towards more financial stability in my life. I was too young to know that pursuing a career in filmmaking left my life to the shoals of instability, chaos, ruin, and poverty. These would take a serious toll on my life and lead me to lose many years, years that I could never reclaim. But it is hard to dissuade someone young and determined. My father tried, on several occasions, failing each time. It must have hurt him inside to see me taking a path that offered few rewards (great for those that achieve success) and much more pain and frustration.

Meanwhile, I kept working. There was a steady pattern to my life that, although frustrating for me, brought stability. And since I was socially pent-up, well, there were the available servers. Not my first choice in dating, but certainly an available one that, at the time, offered no uncomfortable discussion about the son of the owner hitting on the restaurant's attractive waitresses. Eventually this stretched to trying to charm attractive female customers. There was failure, with few exceptions. Work was the central element of my life; back bending, sweaty, leg-sore, aching work that left every part of my body exhausted beyond anything I had ever experienced before, or since. Only now looking back can I reflect on the physical punishment I endured, a punishment known to most of ordinary society in developing countries, and throughout the history of our race—that most worked and continue to do so now like dogs, while a few rest on their wealth. My work could hardly compare to the slaves of the past, but I had tasted enough of this physical punishment to know it was unendurable. No human can sustain that kind of daily grind and survive, yet billions have, and they continue to do so today.

Nothing prepared me for this work. Even my father never knew what it was like to sweat over the kitchen moving at 100 mph to make a breakfast dish. I don't recall that he ever worked an entire shift as a cook in his entire forty years at the restaurant. I never knew myself to be capable of it, nor to rise to the speed and physical endurance that cooking on the front lines demanded, and it surprised me. I think it surprised

No one could charm them like Demetre Lagos, a natural, buoyant figure in the eatery and a friend to all. For many, it was "Demetre's," not the Continental.

everyone in the family, since I was known as an "egghead," not a working stiff. Yet, here I was, outshining everyone. Where did this work ethic come from? To this day, I do not know. Perhaps it was the sheer pressure of having to satisfy all those customers and knowing that the livelihood of the entire family depended on me that forced me to take on the role with gusto. At the end of each shift, as weary and spent as I was, there was a certain nobility to my efforts. I had done it. We, Carol and I, worked as a great team and made it through another busy shift.

And so it was for my entire college career. I do not recall much of my college days, but I do vividly reflect on my days at the Conti. There was never a dull moment. One of my father's new partners, someone we had known in church, had his wife and daughter occasionally helping at the restaurant. Helping usually meant that they stood in the "front" (the dining area) seating customers, taking care of the register (I am using restaurant lingo here—this refers to ringing up the customers' bills and taking payment), handling solicitors, answering the phone, and helping the wait staff when the restaurant got slammed (busy). They also helped out during one of the "fun" events of the year for the Conti—the University District Street Fair.

Begun in 1969 as a way to bring the community together, but to also promote the arts and culture of the local area, the Street Fair swelled with hipness and a hip vibe. Today it is mostly corporate, but at the time, it really was a celebration of community that attracted tens of thousands of people—particularly families and students from the adjacent university. As the Continental was a business on the Ave, we were allowed to set up a booth directly in front of our restaurant. In our case, this meant a few grills, some dispensers and ice to sell soda and plenty of wine bottles to sprinkle on the cooking souvlaki (shish kebab) skewers on the grill. But for me, it was a chance to ogle the many attractive young women who wandered by.

Like my cooking work on the weekends, the three days of the festival were busy, and we went through thousands of souvlakis, gyros, and chicken skewer sandwiches. It was during my second year of manning the booth that the daughter of the partner was assigned the role of cashier. There were usually three of us on the grill line (Carol, myself, and another cook) for the greater part of the day—usually from ten in the morning to about seven in the evening, by which time the crowds had slackened considerably. We yelled, we screamed, we sang, we laughed, we joked—we had great fun. All the while we worked as hard as ever—in assembly line fashion—as one worked the grill, the other put on the condiments, and the third made sure everything was stocked. The system worked well. Throughout all this the partner's daughter took cash (back when it was the norm) and gave change, and so forth for three days.

27

It was a restaurant and pastry shop, but also a grocery store and wine shop, and it even sold Greek coffee pots ("brikia"). This combination bothered few.

Then when it came time to count the proceeds on Monday, we were shocked to find out that sales were down considerably from the previous years. It was stunning, considering that the amount of food served was the same as before. So, what could account for the difference? Since there were no receipts given to customers (this is no longer the case now), there was no way to account for the missing sales. Yet, we had the receipts for the meat ordered so we knew how many sandwiches (a loose term, since they were not sandwiches in the traditional sense, but pita, meat, and condiments all wrapped together) we gave out. My father became an investigator as he pored over the records to solve the mystery.

The more he thought about it, the more he realized what had happened. The facts stared him in the face. I didn't know exactly what was on his mind, but he did not seem happy for weeks after the festival. He knew something serious had occurred that could not be ignored. I found out about the confrontation after the fact, but essentially he realized there had been a theft. Money was missing, and there was only one

28

person that could account for it—the partner's daughter. My father met with the partner and related the facts to him—the amount of meat and pita bread sold (knowing how many pitas were sold gave us an exact count of how many sandwiches were produced) and the sales that could not account for it. The evidence was simply overwhelming, and my father demanded to know how his daughter could account for the missing sales. The partner apparently had no answer but would speak to his daughter about it.

I always considered the partner to be a nice, friendly old man who was a bit dowdy and absent-minded, but essentially decent. His wife was a bit sharper on the edges, with a bright smile but a stinging temper, so I kept my distance from her. Around the restaurant, the word had spread about unaccounted sales. I was removed from the gossip networks at the time, so I was not sure what exactly was being said. I asked Carol about it, but she just shook her head painfully, muttering, "Let's wait and see what happens."

The truth came not long afterwards. The daughter confessed to stealing several thousands of dollars of cash. Perhaps the word "confessed" is not the right term. I think by that time, my father was so angry that he was going to call the police to investigate the matter. So, one day the partner came to my father and told him what happened—his daughter was short of money and decided to help herself. When I learned this, I suddenly remembered that several times throughout the day the daughter went to the bathroom, which struck me as odd. The others went perhaps two or three times to the bathroom, but every two or three hours, she claimed she had to go. It all made sense—she was simply using that excuse to hide the cash.

My father gave the partner an ultimatum—either he sell his portion of the restaurant, or the police would be notified about the theft. Interestingly, my dad did not demand the money back. The partner decided to sell his portion, and thus it came to be that in a few months my father became the proud and sole owner of the Continental Greek Restaurant and Pastry Shop.

In any cash business, it is always tempting to slip some bills in one's pocket. It is hard to fathom now, given that we live in an electronic world where cash is getting rarer, but at the time, credit card use was small compared to cash and checks (we had a huge problem with checks that returned with insufficient funds). The original partner tried to teach my brother how to skim profits without detection (I was in the office when this lesson was attempted). I was shocked by this revelation, and

I wondered how many other restaurateurs fell for this theft. Years later, when I participated in the Bite of Seattle, I witnessed a restaurant owner doing the same with his cash sales, so I got my answer—it seems many do. I don't know if this is possible today, but it was probably common at the time we took over the Conti.

Within a few years my father had gone from being a plumber to a reluctant restaurant partner, and now he owned the operation completely on his own. Can anything better explain the meaning and reality of America better than this? No longer would he have to deal with the machinations of partners, or thieving daughters, or not being able to resolve differences. He was his own boss, and with my brother as manager, it became a full-fledged family affair.

His problems had just begun.

CHAPTER TWO

Rise of the Greek Restaurateur

If anything needed change, it was the kitchen. The crammed affair had taken its toll on Carol and me. She decided to retire, and eventually I would leave as well, so the problem could no longer be avoided. My father was not an architect (my brother had wanted to be one when he was young), but he consulted my brother as well as a local restaurant service firm. They pored over the problem and realized that the big issue was that the kitchen was too small to handle the flow of orders. It also had to be separated from the walkway so as to reduce the visitors who impeded our cooking by passing through. Redesigning the kitchen is not as simple as one might imagine. It requires not only the usual paperwork with the city, but also having to realign water and power lines, drill holes through the roof for the venting system, and move the refrigerators to make the kitchen work properly. What seemed like a job that could be done in a few months turned into a multi-year project.

One thing that restaurants abhor is alteration. To change some element of a restaurant is to take the operation from one set of functions to another. And even if the change is a vast improvement, it jars the usual flow of the operation. Since restaurant work is so entirely physical, muscle memory can make transitions difficult. Even us cooks, who knew the old kitchen was not sustainable and made life so difficult for us, wearily regarded the impending changes. We would have to get used to a new set of muscle memories, and this was daunting.

My father was steadfast in his determination to replace the old kitchen. There would be some disruption, to be sure, but he knew implicitly that there was no choice—the restaurant was not an efficient operation with the old kitchen. Cooks needed more space to do their tasks, with the greater and easier flow that came with it. The question also arose of how to pay for it. As a small ethnic restaurant, the Conti had an adequate cash flow (I did not have access to the accounting books, so I relied on what my father told me about the situation and what I heard in conversations), but it wasn't great. That would come a few years later.

My father was still paying back his bank loan for his share of the restaurant, and on top of it, a disagreement with my uncle (with whom the family stayed from the time we arrived in the U.S.) led to us fleeing to our own place. We left Uncle John's palatial, seaside home (with a tennis court, not bad for an immigrant dentist), and went to a tiny apartment that was several notches down from the space we had gotten used to. It was owned by a Russian exile who had written a play about Joseph Stalin (claiming his death was due to poisoning) and believed in miracles (showing X-rays where he had been healed after a special prayer). It was from that tiny apartment that I completed my college career, while still cooking at the restaurant.

The big story of the time was my mother deciding to help out at the Conti. This came as a big surprise to everyone in the family, most

Demetre Lagos became knowledgeable about wines over the years, and he drew in a wine-appreciating clientele. It was one of the unexpected discoveries: a simple Greek restaurant could also serve and sell outstanding wines.

especially my father. My mother's story is a compelling one, and one that says much about Greek America. Throughout this book so far you have noticed that the focus has been almost exclusively on my father, and for the obvious reasons—it was his purchase that led the family into a new profession. My brother, I, and even later on my sister came to participate. In fact, there was no finer server in the history of the restaurant than my sister. Perhaps I might even venture to say she was the finest server I have ever encountered in my life. So, what was my mother doing during this period?

Let me backpedal a moment here. Like most Greek mothers, when I was born, her role in a patriarchal society was to run the household and raise us children. My father had his labor during the day, and when it was completed, he trotted off to the *kafenia* in the evenings, while the rest of us stayed home. My grandmother lived with us, and there was never a shortage of company to keep us entertained (this was before television). So, it was not a big deal that my father spent the evenings at the *kafenia*, playing poker, arguing politics, keeping up with the latest news and gossip in the village. But I always felt that my mother resented the greater freedom that he had, that the responsibility of raising the family fell on her. I have no evidence to back up this point; it is simply an observation. I was too young and carefree to be concerned; I had my friends, I had my school, I had my own battles to face.

When we came to the United States, the surprise in those early days was that my mother was pregnant. Six months after our arrival, there was a new baby girl in the family. That kept my mother—and, for a while, me—busy for a few years, but eventually my sister grew up into a confident, strong-willed personality. She loved cooking and baking, and our house was always filled with the aroma of her latest creation. This was starting from the age of eight. I was busy reading *Sports Illustrated*; she read *Gourmet*.

It was many years later that I realized all of us in the family (except perhaps my sister, the only one born in the United States) had to undergo a shift. Mine was not a pleasant one; I had loved and was used to the environment in the village and coming to America unnerved me. It was not just the new food, new atmosphere, new climate, new culture, and new language that bothered me—it was that my routine was disrupted, that I no longer had my best friend George, and that the entire village had been my backyard to play in, whereas in America this no longer existed. The transition was indeed cruel. Everything about those first two years were painful. I often cried coming back from school. I

Beginning in the late 1980s, the restaurant set up food booths at local out-door food festivals that became hugely popular in Seattle. This one was at the Bite of Seattle.

was learning the language fast enough, I suppose (stringing phrases together), but it was a slow process; I had no friends, I was isolated in school (the only foreigner), now shunted to the sidelines of the elementary school. Once I even told my mother, through bitter tears, that I would walk back to Greece to leave this wretched place!

Assimilation came to me slowly. A kind gesture here and lucky break there, and soon I was able to master the language, two more years to feel comfortable writing it, and then eventually to feel a part of the culture in fits and starts. It was hardly a smooth process, and it seemed every day I learned something new. (I still remember scratching my head when someone told me to get off his back. I politely told him that I was not on his back, to which the boy cracked up laughing!) My brother had an easier time of it; he came to seventh grade from Greece, found a best friend, was friendly with girls (who liked him), and generally sailed through the changeover with ease.

And what was my mother doing this whole time? She cared for the house, which means the big house we lived in with Uncle John. It was not the first residence we lived in when we arrived in the U.S. We first lived in a crammed apartment, The Viking, and later moved to a small house next to a plumbing company with a big lawn. Then a year later was the shift to a huge house next to the water and railroad tracks. It had a swimming pool, and later Uncle John built a tennis court. He was doing well, and he wanted to show off. I never really thought much of the house but living there did make us popular with the Greek American community for which such status symbols really matter.

Yet she was the one cleaning the big house and raising us kids. It was enormous and frustrating work for her, without any help. She had asked for such help, but it never came. Moving to our own place resulted from her frustration at being regarded as a maid, which grated on her, as it would on anyone. It was her desire to have our own place that finally pushed my father to do so. The move was several steps down from our previous position, and whispers began in the Gram (Greek American) community as to what that meant. For the four-year period we were in the flat we kept a low profile. I got my driver's license and promptly smashed into another car only a few days afterwards.

Moving to the apartment gave my mother a newfound sense of freedom and confidence. By this point, my sister was a precocious eight-year-old, and it seemed my mother wanted to explore new landscapes. Unlike my father, she never learned to speak or write English. My father had special tutoring lessons when we first arrived in the United States, but this privilege was not extended to my mother. True, this was based on the need of my father to learn to speak the language since he was already employed as a plumber (in the company located next to the house), but it seemed a slight that I am sure pained my mother.

Sometime after moving into the flat, my mother told my father her desire to help out at the restaurant. I don't know my father's reaction, since I was not there at the time of the discussion. As was the case with many things, I learned about the matter afterwards. My mother felt cooped up in the apartment, and she was getting tired of watching soap operas. It was exciting at first for her to watch TV, something we had never done before moving to America, but it didn't fulfill her social needs. I don't remember the exact day my mother started appearing at the restaurant, but when she did it was a revelation. Prior to this, she expressed her desire to get a driver's license. Most other Gram women she knew had learned to drive and why not her? It fell upon me to teach her. Either I was a terrible teacher or she a terrible student, or some combination of the two, but after a few lessons I gave up.

In blunt language that I now regret, I told her she was a menace being on the road, and she stopped speaking to me for a while. A Gram family friend decided to help, and she seemed happy with him, so in a few months she was ready for her exams—both the written and the driving tests. No problem with the second, but she flunked the first. Her command of English was negligible. She grew frustrated and didn't know what to do.

The family social network came to the rescue, in particular one man we will call Peter. He had some Greek ancestry in him and was one of the singularly most vital, unique, and incredible characters I have ever met in my life. An accident as a youngster left him with a permanent limp, but nothing stopped his vitality. He was the owner of the plumbing company that employed my father (and it was his house that Uncle John rented). Apparently, he and my uncle had been friends for some time. That friendship proved vital. Sometime in the early 1970s he travelled with his family to Greece to get in touch with his roots, back when it was popular to do so. He brought back a Super 8 movie of his visit to the village that I can still vividly remember. Giving employment to my father was a bit of a risk, but in another way, it was smart business. My father was an exceptionally hard worker and one that squirmed at nothing.

Peter was such a vivacious personality, and he knew everyone of substance in the community. He had two lovely daughters, one of whom I fell in love with, and I never knew him to be anything other than jovial and happy. Truly, he was an exceptional human being who in his largess, physique, and joviality reminded me of the original medieval version of Santa Claus. He heard about my mother's plight and went immediately to work. He had a friend in Wenatchee who happened to be a driver's license official with the Washington State Department of Motor Vehicles. I do not know the exact nature of what happened next, but all I know is that one fine Saturday morning, my mother announced that Peter was taking her to Eastern Washington for a short excursion. I provide the PG version of the story; I think my father was jealous that she was taking the trip with a man other than himself. Needless to say, she returned with the news that she passed her written test. How this happened my mother would not say, to this day.

The restaurant represented the second step in her goal of liberation. I later wondered where this desire came from. It was telling that one of her fondest memories of the restaurant was the afternoon that Gloria Steinem came to dine with a friend. It was the first time that I realized my mother must've been a strong proponent of greater female participation and freedom in society. It never occurred to me that she could be anything else but my mother. The myopia of kids.

But the restaurant was a different matter than obtaining a driver's license. She spoke little English. She could not write it. What exactly would be her role? By the time I left for Los Angeles in 1981 to pursue a film career, I would not be around to find out. But in my frequent trips back home, it was becoming more obvious—she had become a server. And not just an ordinary server—an exceptionally efficient one and the favorite of many customers. She became a "borrowed" mom to many young men (some of them members of rock bands). She knew what her customers wanted and brought it to them without any more words exchanged than "Good morning." Slowly and steadily, she learned to speak English and even to write it (as was necessary when taking orders). Her handwriting to this day leaves something to be desired,

There were comical moments, too. Here we have two non-smoking tables surrounded by smokers. Did the smoke suddenly stop at the non-smoking tables? The absurdity of this quickly became obvious and it was the intervention of Katerina Lagos that put an end to the ridiculousness.

but it was good enough to be read by the steady stream of cooks that paraded through the kitchen.

In time, she began to exert her influence on the operation, showing her management skills as well. Up until this point it was easy to assume that the Conti was my father's "place," but the reality was no longer accurate. It belonged as much to my mother and brother as to my father. The signatures and contracts indicated otherwise, but the reality was different. A historian conducting research on Gram restaurants might look at the restaurant's legal paperwork and assume that it was another father-dominated operation and yet miss the full picture and impact that my mother had on the restaurant. Is this true of other Gram operations? I suspect this is the case but can offer little evidence for it.

My mother checked the hours recorded by all the employees to sniff out any irregularities, and she managed the front part of the operation with hawk-like diligence; she kept an eye on the other servers, making sure they did not spend too much time on their breaks, and, sometimes frustratingly for others, especially me when I was cooking, made sure we never gave out more than the right number of Greek fries on the breakfast plates. It was breathless to see this transformation. In time, customers came to appreciate her skills more than my father's, which I think he resented. For many customers, she was the face of the Conti, and a steadying force on the entire operation. When accidents happened—a flooded pipe in the back of the restaurant, a broken deep-fryer in the kitchen, a busted dishwashing machine—it was my mother who calmed everyone and kept the situation from exploding. When the restaurant was finally sold, I don't remember that she had any particular emotion about it, although I know inside she hurt because she would miss her coterie of friends.

Her appearance at the restaurant was good for business. She had her devoted customers, and breakfast was an especially important time for the operation. She worked the morning and lunch shift before heading home. Breakfast was the key item on weekends, when Carol and I worked, and the trick was to enlarge the breakfast business during the week. Doing that meant increased business. I am not clear on the details of how my father eventually came to pay for the kitchen remodel (whether he took out a bank loan for the restaurant or paid the remodeling company in installments), but he managed to do so. My mother was establishing herself as the premier server (when my sister was not working), and this translated into bigger breakfast sales on weekdays.

Lunch and dinner also needed revamping, and in time they too came to my father and brother's attention. By revamping I mean that dishes had to be dropped, new ones added, old dishes made new, and dish preparations changed. If this sounds easy it is not. There is a science to the process, which I am not entirely sure I understand (I have not gone through a culinary school like the Culinary Institute of America). It is similar to making movies; it is not easy to always to predict which films will become box-office hits. Customers' tastes shift and parry, and keeping up with them, or staying ahead of them, keeps many restaurant consultants busy. We did not have the revenues to support any outside consultations, so all changes had to be done within the confines of the family.

The CIA teaches these skills to its students, not to ethnic restaurateurs like my father, who had to make do with his native good sense. He had an intuitive feel for what customers might like and much of the time he was right. Not always. When he tried to introduce real feta (that is to say, not made out of cow's milk but goat's and sheep's milk), it was a disaster. Similar to changing from Greek fries (round-shaped) to hash browns, customers rebelled. One of them even came back to the kitchen and threatened my father with death if he did not revert to the original Greek fries. He was joking, but my father didn't need further explanation. We went back to the Greek fries.

Kenneth Clark, in his brilliant *Civilisation* series for BBC-TV, called the great inventor and personal hero of mine Thomas Alva Edison a "supreme do-it-yourself man," and he was right.[1] My father was in the same vein. Perhaps most Gram restaurateurs are. He did everything at the restaurant on his own without any real guidance except his own skill and wisdom. For many, it is the only way to survive. If utilizing (or exploiting) family members keeps costs low, so does becoming the main handyman to the operation. My father could fix, most of the time, broken ovens, dishwashers, and refrigerators. Only when he got too old to do so did he assign the tasks to professional repairmen (in all the years at the restaurant I never once saw a female repairperson; I hope that this is changing).

None of us in the family, when we entered the restaurant business, had any clue that we followed in the great tradition of tens of thousands of other Gram restaurateurs. We simply had no idea. It meant little to us at the time, except that many of us asked us why we did so. The answer was simple: because my father took advantage of an opportunity. He borrowed $25,000 from the bank, which took him many years to repay, and the rest is family history. We were also asked why so many Greeks entered the business, a question no doubt posed to other ethnic groups and certain professions that they came to dominate—i.e., Koreans and grocery stores, Chinese and laundromats, etc. The answer is surprisingly complex.

In Gergely Baics's fascinating *Feeding Gotham*, Baics recounts the shift from the city provisioning markets—where meats, fish, and produce were sold—as being the responsibility of local government to one that was increasingly taken over by economic market forces.[?] It was a seismic shift that local government no longer would operate such markets but leave it to private industry to do so. The shift took place after the 1820s, at a time of the industrializing cityscape. Removing local authority (expect in matters of hygiene, licensing, and regulation) from such popular markets gave primacy to businesspeople who directly responded to customers' tastes. New York City is the particular focal point for the rise of ethnic restaurants, since it was the largest urban center in the country with the most immigrants—and, it turns out, a petri dish of experimentation.

The great Second Wave of immigrants into the United States began in the 1880s, and before it was over in 1924, 22.5 million foreigners had swept onto our shores, the largest such influx percentage-wise ever in the nation's history, and one that severely transformed the nation into a polyglot of ethnicities, the effects of which, it must be added, echo in today's culture. As I mentioned earlier, one of the cultural attributes that Greeks brought to their new land was the community center/café, the *kafeneion*. It provided stability, gossip, camaraderie, exchange, and other social lubricants vital for the emerging Gram community's survival. It was not a far stretch to go from *kafeneion* to restaurant, since profits were greater. So was the work commitment, which meant cooks, dishwashers, servers, etc., which meant employment for family members and friends. How many successful entrepreneurs in America got their start as a dishwasher in a Greek restaurant? I don't know the exact figure, if any really exists, but I can only guess it is a quite a large number. My own family gave many arriving immigrants to Seattle from the Middle East and Eastern Europe jobs as cooks or dishwashers at the restaurant.

One key factor to entry into the restaurant business was relatively low costs. In 1974, $25,000 (or about $130,000 today) was not insignificant.[3] Had he wanted to, my father could have avoided the bank loan and simply gone to members of the Gram community in Seattle for the funds. A thrifty Greek immigrant in the 1880s in New York City who dreamed of his own business could have done the same, and many did. The point is that the entry barrier to owning a restaurant was not insurmountable. If one Greek could do it, others followed.

It was not a profession that required extensive schooling or specialized degrees; mainstream professions such as medicine, dentistry, law, and engineering required extensive schooling. Since many Greek immigrants came from rural backgrounds with little education, the obstacles to their entry were formidable. We may say that these professions were "closed" to these foreigners, not in the legal sense, but simply out of practicality. In time the children of these immigrants became doctors, lawyers, dentists, and engineers, but not at the turn of the twentieth century when these aliens were merely trying to survive in a hostile land.

Even as nativists derided the newcomers, the undeniable reality was that they brought with them a wonderful new cuisine that offered variety to urban dwellers and whetted their appetites. Like other ethnic immigrants had done and would do following the Second Wave, Greeks brought new tastes and new dishes into a culture that was ripe for their exploitation. Urban patrons sought out ethnic food because it was tasty, cheap, and, in places like New York, Boston and Chicago, common. Southeastern Europeans, like Greeks and Italians, were derided as "garlic eaters," because with the use of so much fresh garlic in their cuisine, it emanated from their skin and mouths, yet these same folks brought unique variety to the American food landscape. My father had no culinary background before buying into the Conti, but no one could beat him in his garbanzo beans and chicken dish, or his lamb and baked potatoes. To an American palate not used to such exotic dishes, it proved a revelation. It still does today. No one foresaw that Greeks would come to dominate restaurants and diners; it is tempting to think of a conspiracy, but none existed. It is a matter of one element leading to the next, and in time thousands of Greek restaurants appeared across the land.

I tracked a similar story with immigrants' involvement in the emerging film business in the early 1900s in my book *American Zeus*.[4] Alexander Pantages (born Pantazis) was a Greek immigrant who ran away from his family's home on Andros to seek his fortune. He landed in the United States sometime in the 1880s and eventually, after a circuitous path, took over a stage theater in Dawson City, Yukon, during the Alaska Gold Rush days. In 1902, he opened his first theater in Seattle, the Crystal, which offered vaudeville acts as well as movies at a time when films were just a couple of minutes long and without any

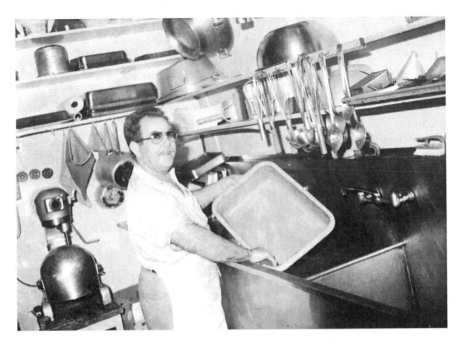

George Lagos was never too proud to wash dishes, fix plugged toilets or repair the big pastry oven. He was a jack of all trades, and his enthusiasm and commitment never wavered for 40 years.

connecting storyline or purpose. Thousands of other immigrants across the country followed his example.

It required relatively few funds to open up such an operation (a typical storefront theater had a bunch of old chairs, a simple stage, a bed sheet for a screen, and used a projector) and little skill, except the ability and desire to work hard. Pantages was his own manager, ticket taker, janitor, usher, and projectionist. Labor overhead was low and the possibility of profit high. And this attracted immigrants—Greeks, Italians, Jews—to the emerging film business.

There was another factor, which is perhaps true of restaurants as well—many Anglo-Americans refused to get involved in movies, which they considered second-rate, or even worse, entertainment. This opened the door for immigrants, and they jumped through. In time, these immigrants came to dominate the movie industry and with it came exhortations by nativists that "alien hordes" had conspired to take over the nation's "dream factories," as Hollywood studios were called. And with it came the divisive culture wars that still poison our culture.

Chapter Two. Rise of the Greek Restaurateur

Many Anglo-Americans did not want to go into the service indus-try like restaurants. First, it was a "feminine" industry, and second, there was nothing appealing about its strenuous work schedule. It was left up to immigrants who had relatively few choices of employment to fill the gap and a willingness to work hard since muscle they had in abundance, but few higher skills.

My father never got beyond the sixth grade before World War II killed his education. My mother stopped in the fourth grade. Like mil-lions of other immigrants before them, they were low-skilled workers limited in their choices of what professions they could pursue. Only with luck and a willingness to take a risk did my father find himself as the proud owner of his own business that presented headaches and chal-lenges on a daily basis. The long hours, the surly customers, the pressure to perform during rushes, the many ways that things could go wrong all weighed on him. And the rest of the family. We were at the behest of forces beyond our control and no plans, however ingenious, could bar-ricade us from catastrophe and disaster. Employees could quit suddenly, food could be served with hair in it, the entire refrigerator system could suddenly collapse, or, before the installation of air conditioning, a heat wave could turn the entire restaurant into an extension of the big oven we had.

When I wonder what kept my father going, I am sure it was the same as millions of other immigrants—there was simply no choice. There was only the restaurant; what could he do otherwise? Go back to plumbing? The lack of options provided my father and the family with a steely determination not available to others and which kept everyone going for nearly forty years.

By 1980 there was a noticeable uptick in business at the Conti. The updated and upgraded dishes had made a difference, as had the new kitchen that streamlined the entire cooking process. It had taken some time to get used to, but less than originally feared. Cooks loved it. I loved it. There was room for maneuvering, stocking items were within easy reach, stacked dishes were near our prep area, and there was plenty of grill space, which had previously limited our ability to produce the cooked items for the dishes. And, perhaps most importantly, two cooks could work in the space, whereas before it was tight with one, impossi-ble with two. No longer. It made cooking a joy.

I was coming to the end of my college career and a decision had to be made as to what I wanted for my life. I did not fancy myself a cook or imagine working at the restaurant the rest of my life. That much I knew, although in retrospect I had no good reason not to other than I did not like the work. My sister was a natural, and if anyone should have carried on the family tradition it was she, but she too had other ideas. I still clambered for movies, and, blindly, I followed this path. A year after graduating from college, I had been accepted into the graduate program of the University of Southern California's famed film school and decided to move to Los Angeles. I had told my brother of my plans, and he seemed supportive, although I think he felt sad that I would be leaving. He and I did not always get along or see the restaurant business the same way, but we still had a mutual love and respect that broke through disagreements. My father was very angry and hurt when I told him the news. My mother cried.

Time gives us the ability to reflect on decisions; I can honestly say now that the move to Los Angeles brought joy and pain into my life and set it on an entirely different course than what I expected. I do not regret the decision; I had to go and see the world, even if I was not prepared for it. It brought me closer to myself and with it came painful lessons in life. What would have happened had I remained? Likely in time I might have had my own restaurant and the dignity and hardships that came with it. Whether I might be happier is another matter, but I would certainly have lived a much more stable life than what took place with my transfer to LA. The profound sense that my life was a continual rollercoaster, or a surf ride on a wild wave, left its mark on my sensibility that I have never quite gotten over. I could deride the restaurant life as one of continual problems punctuated by tiny moments of joy and pride, but I was simply too young to appreciate the fruits that it could have provided me.

CHAPTER THREE

Through Bad Times
and Good

If I thought I would escape the restaurant business by moving to Los Angeles, I was sadly mistaken. I would labor for several years at the Old World Restaurant on the corner of Sunset Boulevard and Holloway Drive in West Hollywood.[1]

It was a long drive to my new home. I packed up the AMC Hornet with all my clothes, got $700 from my mother who stood in front of the garage door of the new home my father had purchased as she waved goodbye to me, wishing me the best of luck. The drive down I-5 was uneventful, and only when I headed to the Oregon coast did the scenery change and my mood brighten. The beauty of the place was not just breathtaking, but almost spiritual. Years later I would come back to Heceta Beach, near Lincoln City, and be mesmerized by the huge sandy beach and the raucous waves. It was surreal, stunning, yet serene. I didn't have a chance to stop the car and get out as I did on my return journey, but I made a mental note of the place.

I stopped at a roadside motel in southern Oregon, waking up the next morning and continuing. It was June, and the weather was pleasant and delightful. The drive down the coast of California was like nothing I had ever witnessed before, or since. All the while I wondered if I had made the right decision. I had a friend's house to stay in for a few days, but otherwise no prospects other than film school to start in autumn. What lay before me was a huge question mark, a sword that would hang for decades to come. Big Sur was a revelation, and although I plugged along at an even but slow pace, passed by other more intrepid souls, I was content to just take in the scenery. I knew Big Sur was responsible for preventing many suicides, and I could see why. It is the curious mixture of coastline, ocean, beach, sun, and glimmering water that makes it such a gorgeous site. I cannot think of a more beautiful place in the entire world than Big Sur. I only saw it one more time in all the years I

45

lived in Los Angeles, but I made enough mental pictures to carry me to this day.

As I continued my sojourn south, the terrain seemed more and more familiar—the rocky desert, wind-swept landscape that clearly brought back memories of Greece and its crusted earth. A cascade of warmth settled on me, as if I had entered comfortable and familiar territory. In a way, I had. Two years prior to the move, I had driven with a girlfriend down to Los Angeles to spend a few days, so it was not completely unknown to me. The difference here was that this was no longer just a visit, but a new home. Yet, even though I had prepared for this moment for some months now, it never felt real. Even on the long drive south. Not, that is, until I turned off California Highway 1 and found myself on I-10 did it finally become reality.

If the terrain was familiar, the city was not. This was not Seattle, but

George Lagos's ritual was the same: work for twelve hours per day, no days off (except Thanksgiving, Christmas and New Year's), then in the evenings go to the front pastry side and spend time with the many friends of the eatery. In such moments are life's meanings made. Berndt Schmidt and Russell Valley are on the right. Vidya Ramdin and Ted Neal are at left.

several Seattles, all bundled together into a heaving, buzzing, intense package. From a distance LA (or "El Aye" as some called it then) was merely a spider's web of freeways and highways that traversed a huge swath of land. It's hard to call it a city, but more like a flat expanse of buildings defined by no boundaries or barriers or limits. This was the opposite of New York: congested, but in size, not in density. Los Angeles did not demand understanding, but immersion. It was like a giant ant colony that kept moving and heaving and pointed to all directions without regard to rules or regulations (I believe in the jungle this kind of colony is called a "grex"). And now I was part of this pulsating mass, one ant in a big carpet of millions of other ants set to march to the rhythm and flow of the colony. And I was terrified.

I had left the comforts of my home to get out of my forsaken bubble but had landed in a cauldron of intensity that I was clearly not prepared for. Forget the film career at the moment; what occupied my mind was survival. How would I stay alive in such a place? What would I do? How would I compete against the millions of other movie hopefuls that filled the city to the brim? I had no clue and would not even know where to begin. For the first time in the journey, I wanted to cry. But I had no time. Using directions, I found my way to the Silver Lake area and my friend's house (really, my friend's friend's house). Within one week I would have to find my own place. Life reduced to basics.

The restaurant and Seattle now seemed like a long-ago dream. I regretted leaving and realized I had made a huge mistake, but it was too late to go back now. The damage was done, and I had to pick up the pieces. And how painful it was to recover the many pieces of this awful decision. Each night I went to bed with a huge searing knot in my belly, only to wake up the next morning with the knot still there. The few days at the house had made my anxiety worse, not better, and when I had to find my own flat, I saw my meager saved funds dwindling rapidly. My girlfriend was then in Paris pursuing a modeling career (I had paid for her airline ticket), and I called her to see if she would come back so we could live together. That would happen several months later, in the meantime, I had to find work. The same friend who arranged for me to live with his friend suggested I contact a "boiler-room" operation selling pencils and pens to organizations around the country. I was given a tiny desk, a sheet with names and phone numbers to contact, and a script to read. I was a terrible salesman. In fact, worse than awful. I felt like a crook, and it no doubt came through in my voice because in the three weeks I was on the job, I do not recall ever getting one sale. Not one.

Cooking Greek, Becoming American

There was another agent in the office who was my opposite—a tall, lanky fellow with a smooth voice that made it seem cool you were talking to a friend. When he got on the phone he was relaxed as a cucumber and as refreshing as sweet iced tea on a hot, muggy day. I often sneaked a peek when he was in action, just to see how he did it. He was rarely turned down. Rarely. And when he was, he just smiled, picked up his cup of coffee, sipped, and went right back to the next one, which he nailed. I was in the presence of the Beethoven of boiler-room sales, and it was a sight to behold.

One day the manager came to my desk, asked me how I was doing, and told me she wanted to see me in her office. I knew what this meant, so I gulped and marched towards the inevitable. It lasted no more than a minute. She was sorry, but she had to let me go because I was not producing any sales. I nodded, holding back tears, and thanked her for giving me the opportunity. I was then twenty-two and knew that there was no future for me in pencils and pens. As I left, I saw the maestro doing his thing on the phone, ringing up another sale. I shook my head painfully and walked out the door. Now what?

My money was rapidly dwindling. Orientation to USC film school was coming up. It took place in a big theater space, with perhaps 150 students there. I even heard two students speaking in Greek. All of us were miniature Spielbergs, and our arrogance showed. Not so much out of any malicious pride, but simply out of carrying a long-held dream that had enveloped our lives. In that moment, I realized the self-absorbed quality of that dream. So why did I want to become a filmmaker—actor, director, or producer? Because I had great stories to tell? Because I could entertain millions and return a profit to my investors? Because I could advance culture, as pompous as that sounded? The reality was I wanted simply to make films because it was, well, so different from reality. Because it was fantasy, and something different than the world that stared me in the face. It was, let's put it this way, an escape for me to enter a world where I was not the victim, or loser, or shy one, or second-class citizen. Did that qualify me to make films? When I realized it didn't, and it happened in the span of that first meeting, the writing on the wall was clear—I did not belong there. I asked an administrator to move me to the producing program, but I was rejected. The reason for which I had come to LA now vanished. It also didn't help that I had no idea how I would even pay the steep tuition film school demanded; I had assumed my family would help me, but my father had no such desire. He considered filmmaking a perfect waste of time and not a profession that

48

anyone with a decent mind would ever pursue. "You're not even Jewish!" he had yelled at me when I asked for financial assistance.

I was not even Jewish.

My money was almost gone, so I had to get a job. Scouring the newspapers, I found a sales job in the "dining circle" (dishes, etc.) of the Bullock's store in the Century City Mall. It paid minimum wage plus commission for some sales. Unlike the boiler-room operation, it was more my style. I flirted with the attractive women, and this helped my sales. The manager of the department came down one day to congratulate me. I met a man in his late sixties who rode a big Harley to work and loved reading biographies and who became a sort of mentor to me. I don't know if he had a family or not; he never spoke of one as such, so I didn't ask, but he knew a lot about history, so we had some interesting discussions of the past. He was calm, erudite, never judgmental, and a damn good salesperson. My style was charm, his was honesty and integrity. I loved to see attractive women come in, most of them Beverly Hills housewives in sweatpants and really expensive pumps, to listen to my charming words and occasional humor. It was schmaltzy, but it worked. I had sales. I was a star. I had a future in retail. Except I hated the job. I hated the cheap, canned music and the whole corporate mentality that pervaded the store. I hated the monotony of selling the same thing over and over again to often rich customers to whom I was just a well-spoken servant there for their entertainment. I never really used my brain on the job, unless you call sexual energy brainwork.

The only respite was the break during my shift when I found myself on a bench in the mall, people watching. One day a man that I took to be in his late twenties or early thirties carrying an expensive attaché case and wearing a three-piece suit came and sat on the bench. After a long pause, he introduced himself. He had a pleasant, cherubic face under a mop of blond hair. I pegged him as a managerial type, but it was hard to know. Maybe he was out interviewing for a job. I don't know. All that I know is that after introducing himself to me, he asked me, "You know what I would really like to do in my life?"

For a moment I froze and wondered if I had wandered into the path of a psycho. I hesitated to answer, but seeing that there were other people about, I reckoned he could not try to kill me without being noticed.

"No," I replied, feebly. "I have no idea."

He looked out at the people hustling around the mall. "I want to get a job working for the FBI for many years, rise up through the ranks, get their complete trust, and then, one day, when I'm the head of the agency, fuck them up real good!"

A strange, beatific smile came over him, one that reminded me of the Mona Lisa at the Louvre. Then, without any warning, he got up and walked away, without even saying goodbye.

When I told my manager, nervously, that I was quitting, she was disappointed. The higher-up that praised my sales came down one day to try to dissuade me, but I told him no. I knew not having a job would imperil me financially, but I had given up on it, and it was not fair to the company for me to stay employed. So as Christmas rolled around, I found myself having little money to buy food and the threat of being homeless. My brother sent me some money to get an airline ticket, and I flew home for the holidays. My girlfriend would arrive after the new year, but until then I had to hang on as best as I could. Christmas was always a busy time at the Conti, and I earned a little helping out in the front (I would never cook again), so that when I left to return to Los Angeles, I had some money to at least eat.

Whatever romantic notion exists around starvation and art completely fades for anyone who has been through this particular horror. It does not spur the creative mind to produce; the only thought that comes to mind under such circumstances is food. I thought a lot about pasta and pizza, ironically. And potatoes. Boiled potatoes. Fried potatoes. Sautéed potatoes. Baked potatoes with oregano and olive oil. Food became an obsession in that period; day and night, I just wanted to eat. I left food plenty to come into starvation, a fact that grew to grate on me with increasing fury.

When my girlfriend arrived, splitting the rent eased my financial burden. She soon got a job as a server at the nearby Old World Restaurant. She managed to talk the manager into also hiring me. So it was, that roughly six months after arriving in Los Angeles to escape the restaurant business, I was right back in it. Not as a cook, fortunately, but as an assistant manager at first, and then, loosely, as an assistant general manager. My time at the Old World was a difficult yet rewarding one; if any singular event changed my life it was this stint. Not only was I introduced, for the first time, to the concept of nutritional food (what we today call "organic"), but I also had to confront my own demons and face growing up, something I had truly avoided all my life.

And there was Gary Jean Philippe.

Our relationship would end bitterly, not on his end, but on mine, but before that, I cannot think of any single human being who has impacted me more than Gary. He was a Haitian immigrant who had arrived in LA at eighteen, and somehow managed to find a position at the Old World buying and delivering produce to its various locations (besides the Sunset location, there was one in Westwood, Palm Springs, and Santa Barbara; a Beverly Hills operation started and later closed). Eventually he rose through the ranks as general manager of the entire company, although I understood the arrangement to be very informal. The restaurant was owned by Dr. Robert I. Franks, dentist to the movie stars, and everything more or less ran informally.

At twenty-three, I had been put into a position of authority and responsibility, and with my girlfriend working at the same time, it seemed an ideal position. I never really thanked her for making this possible, so I had a long way to go to achieve maturity. Even as it sometimes felt like a comedown, working at the Old World provided me many great memories. There was a measure of stability. I could also explore

After he took over the restaurant by himself in 1974, George Lagos in time had to accept the help of his wife, who showed her own amazing adaptability and resilience. She came to manage the front end while George looked after the kitchen. They were an inseparable team, and one that left an impression on all who observed them.

my creativity, as when I started a cable access interview show, *Making America*. I also began writing screenplays. One of them, *Wally's Factory*, caught the attention of an assistant producer at a small Sunset-based production company. She wanted to option the script, but I turned her down (she was not willing to provide any option fee for it). A small production company next to the Old World, Paul Productions, was known to Gary, and not long afterwards they asked me to write a treatment for which I received $500. My life was looking up.

I also found another important outlet that served as a force of stability in my life. Growing up as a child and later as a teenager, I was always chubby. Not quite obese, but rather plump and well-stocked. When a photo of me demonstrating my debating skills was published in the high school annual, I was aghast to see what looked to me like a middle-aged man. I was seventeen at the time. This shocked me, and immediately I decided to lose weight. I changed my diet and began jogging. At first, I would go to the high school track and run laps. Eventually I branched out to long-distance running in the neighborhood. Slowly at first, I began to shed pounds and managed to capture my youth before it completely vanished. It was an important accomplishment for me, and thanks to the help of my girlfriend, I also learned about healthy food. I began to frequent a nutritional store on the Ave. I even fasted for a few days each year. Things got a bit over the top when, at my girlfriend's advice, I opted for a colon cleansing. So, one day I found myself lying on a gurney, a hose attached to my rear end staring at a machine with my own fecal matter passing before my eyes.

Not long after moving to LA I decided to pick up jogging again. I was only a few miles from the University of California, Los Angeles campus. I believe it was an acquaintance at the Old World who told me about people jogging at UCLA's Ducky Drake Stadium in the early morning. A few days later, I found myself at 5:00 a.m. jogging around its beautiful, padded track (one of the first in the nation at the time) with a group of other joggers that I soon realized were regulars. In time, some of them became my friends and my extended family and important anchors in the turbulent years that lay ahead.

The Old World was also an introduction to the culture of Los Angeles. Movie stars of one kind of another paraded through the restaurant. I saw Amy Irving, Danny DeVito, Ashley Judd, and others. One day former governor Jerry Brown came into the Old World to have lunch with a priest. It was heady stuff being able to interact with such luminaries and, yet, all the while, they were simply normal people in a not always normal business. Seeing them, and seeing their decency, made me realize that the normal, the popular conception of the movie industry does not match reality. They came to enjoy the good food in what was once a house, with its "hominess" still intact.

Sunset Boulevard, or the Strip, as our part of the street was called, was a changing place in the 1980s. It still had vestiges of its 1960s heyday—the Whiskey a Go-go, a club west of the restaurant, where many famous rock bands first gained notoriety, and a few blocks east was the Comedy Store that produced many great comedians—yet slowly it was changing. Across from the Old World was Tower Records (it's still there). But directly across from us was a new restaurant that captured the imagination of many leading Angelenos—Wolfgang Puck's Spago. Its main dining area was visible from the street, and for as long as I was at the Old World, I stared in wonder at all the Bentleys, Rolls-Royces, and Mercedes that paraded in and out of the place. It was never not packed. Even the great, German-accented Puck (born in Austria) one day came to the Old World to meet someone, dressed in his chef's uniform. He was short and jovial, but also nervously energetic. I never got the impression that success had swelled his head, but there was a strong sense of confidence about him. He could easily be someone to have a beer with, but he did not seem the type to tell you his nightmares at night.

When I was not working at the Old World and I wanted an escape, my favorite place (sadly now gone) was the Source restaurant a few blocks east. It was part of the hippie movement of the sixties, apparently "LA's First Spiritual Vegetarian Restaurant" that set the standard and inspired many others, perhaps even the Old World.[2] When I entered the Source, I came into the far dimension of an outlier culture. Everything about the place spoke of a bygone era—odd and mismatched tables, slow service, crammed and woody décor—but the spark of the place was its food, particularly its breakfast dishes: pancakes, egg dishes, omelets, with bread that tasted like the sun after a storm. It became a second home to me, and if I could ever own my own eatery, it would imitate the Source.

I knew little of its background, although I knew that it was part of a derisive scene in Woody Allen's *Annie Hall*. The cult Source Family that was behind the effort and its sordid history was not on my radar, and it would probably have mattered very little to me even if it had been, but I simply liked the food. It attracted many film stars from the beginning, "with the likes of Marlon Brando, John Lennon, Warren Beatty, and Julie

Christie as frequent diners."[3] A documentary about the Family was produced in 2012, showing the full effects of the Family's licentiousness.

There was an attraction to the Source that outweighed this past. I suspect that such places represented oases in a society hungering for meaning and spiritual fulfillment that had not been otherwise met. There is a curious pattern to human institutions; they arise to meet specific human needs, yet when those needs go unfilled, new ones are created. The hippie movement and its offshoots, with their emphasis on consuming vegetarian foods, were a reaction to an increasingly commodified culture. It was a childish, permissive, irresponsible movement that left many psychological victims in its wake, but for its adherents it no doubt filled a large void in their lives. I simply loved the food. It opened up a new vista for me that I simply had not known, and I asked myself if Greek food could ever be blended with vegetarianism, or, at least, with nutritional food.

Whenever I returned to the Conti to visit during those LA years, it was always with a sense of disappointment at how traditional its fare was. At the time, for instance, it was common for white bread to be the standard default choice of toasted bread accompanying egg dishes. But wheat bread was better nutritionally for the human body. To make that change required a herculean effort on my part (this happened after I moved back to Seattle).

What grew obvious over time, to my complete surprise, was that I loved Los Angeles. There was a strange vibe to the city, a weird artistic energy that I could not put my finger on, yet one that seemed to me more vital and richer than anything I had ever experienced in Seattle. I met a variety of people in Los Angeles from many places around the globe, attracted to the LA lifestyle, its weather, its movie industry, yet also to a feeling that experimentation was welcome here. Strangely, some of these folks inspired me. One in particular was an artist from Finland. He was tallish, with slightly graying hair, yet I had never seen a man in more perfect physical health than he. In his mid-fifties, he was part of the group of runners at Drake Stadium. Not a jogger, but a runner. I watched him alternate between sprinting and jogging and asked him about it. He said jogging does nothing to your heart, since all it does is let your heart get used to a particular speed. "You need to fool your heart to make it healthy," he told me. "Sprint, slow down, sprint, slow down is the only way to do that," he instructed me in his thick accent.

So, I tried it one day. I almost gasped from exhaustion. It was much harder than regular jogging; I could barely do one lap, while his workout always lasted one hour. There was a lithe female that matched his physical prowess; it was never clear to me if she was an acolyte or a romantic partner. What I did know (thanks to a brief documentary about him on KCET, the local Public Broadcasting System station) was that he lived in the hills above Hollywood and was an artist who produced sculptures. I have tried to repeat this kind of workout in my life a few times, and I have failed each time.

Los Angeles was an entry to a new world, one that I did not know existed. It was a city in deep contrast between richness and poverty, between the slick embrace of status and wealth of Beverly Hills, Brentwood and Santa Monica, and the squalor of East Los Angeles. I could never understand this contradiction in human living, and I never will. I had to put this knowledge away to appreciate the city's rich and world-class art scene (museums, the Getty being the most spectacular) and shopping. I felt like I was in the middle of a real-life Disneyland that still relished pockets of counterculture.

As a resident of West Hollywood, I lived during its official incorporation in 1984 as the first city in the United States to be run by an openly homosexual administration. It was a glorious and historic time for many residents, and we felt the energy that this incorporation emitted. At the time it was fairly easy to get an appointment to meet the staff and elected officials of the city. I had an idea to share with the new city hall, and the staff member listened to my idea: Why not turn the triangular block in front of the restaurant surrounded by Sunset, Holloway and Palm into a park? He regarded me with silence at first, so I had no idea whether he took my notion seriously or not. I explained that the new city could use some more green spaces, and the "parklet" could send an important signal to community residents. We would be different. A sparkle came to his eyes, and a smile. I shut up and did not hear back. But in my first trip back to Los Angeles after returning to live in Seattle, I noticed the parklet there. It has since even been improved upon. My tiny, insignificant contribution to my neighborhood.

And then there were the sudden storms, when suddenly the heavens darkened and gushes of rain were unleashed on the city. Streets became rivers, and for a few hours the city stopped moving. Just as quickly as the torrent had come, it stopped, and the sun emerged. At such moments, I would drive to Mulholland Drive and peer at the washed landscape below, the Pacific Ocean glistening in the distance. The peace, quiet, and serenity of the lookout brought warmth to my soul, much like Big Sur had done when I first moved to the city.

Cooking Greek, Becoming American

The decision to go back to Seattle was not an easy one. I knew that in my seven years in Los Angeles that I had become a sort of man, not fully developed, but well along the way, it seemed. Mistakes lay in the future, but at the time I realized that I could no longer live as a kind of itinerant creator, hoping for my big break, yet seeing the dream recede farther into the distance. And something else—there was a strong racial hostility in the air that had always been there that I had not noticed, but when I did, became palpable in its intensity. LA is a deeply racially divided city, but in the 1980s it probably became more so, and the income inequality bred tension. I felt it the first day I drove to USC to attend orientation. I missed the exit on the freeway and ended up going to Watts to turn around. I saw the misery before my eyes and felt the racial divide when I stopped at a gas station to ask for directions (before the internet and Google Maps). I did not get friendly stares.

My relationship with my girlfriend had come to an end, as had my employment with the Old World. Whatever bites I had in the movie industry came to naught. I flailed about, marking time but not knowing what my next steps should be. Most devastating of all was the end of my relationship with Gary. I knew what it is like to have a brother, but Gary became that and more—perhaps the kind of mentor I wished I always had but never did. My father was always too busy to really have a relationship with me, so I craved the attention of a male figure in my life. Thus, Gary became both my brother and my father, a reliable rock in my life that made me feel quite close to him. It's odd to think that someone from a place I never really knew about—Haiti—could play such an instrumental part in my life. He could not have been more than five years my senior, but in many ways, he was decades ahead of me. He had a grounding of life that took many years for me to appreciate, and a way with people that was pure a reflection of his thoughtful and reflective nature.

I spent time at his house, I got to know his two brothers, and I felt close enough to feel part of his family. There was an implicit understanding of one another; he looked after me while I did his bidding. But life at the Old World grew increasingly complicated as the owner, Dr. Franks, seemed to slide ever deeper into dementia. I was tasked with doing inventory of all the liquor sales, which meant knowing the price of each bottle of liquor on the premises and determining how much was sold. To do this meant poring over all the invoices to determine the prices. This was not easy to do, as there was no filing system to give me all the invoices to gauge the prices (before computerization). So, I began to make up prices to complete the task. I did it once out of expediency and soon it became a monthly habit. When the deception was caught, I had to be punished. Gary would not, could not have fired me, but he let it be known that my situation with the company had changed. I knew the writing was on the wall, and one day I simply stopped working. It was an ignoble end to what had been up to that point had been the purest relationship of my life. And with it came the end of my stay in Los Angeles. Not with a bang, but a whimper.

Rumors circulated that the apartment building where I rented a small space was to be taken over by Paramount Studios and the street closed. I would not wait around for this to happen (it did; the Valentino Building is now part of Paramount). I shipped my things to Seattle in 1989 and found myself living back at home.

And working at the Continental again.

CHAPTER FOUR

Restaurants at the Center of My World

The 1980s were good years for the Continental. The upgrade to the kitchen and the menu, the addition of my mother, and my sister increasingly taking a role in the operation led to more business. Changes to the Ave itself also helped. Often in discussions about the success of an eatery, little is made of the impact the surrounding stores have on business. I am not simply speaking about "location, location, location" as an arbiter of success, but the general quality of the street and neighborhood also contribute to the success or failure of an operation.

The University District in which the Conti was housed has had its ups and downs. Like much of Seattle, it was a distinct neighborhood with its own unique history and image.[1] Originally settled by Duwamish natives perhaps as early as 10,000 years ago, the area supported several small villages that offered land, produce, and game, as well as fishing in the nearby lakes (Lake Union, Lake Washington, Portage Bay). White settlers began arriving after 1867, and by 1890 the area had come to be known as "Brooklyn." In 1891, it was annexed to the city of Seattle. The key event to the area, however, was the extension of electric trolley tracks from downtown to "University Station," as it became more commonly known. In spiderweb-like fashion, tracks also connected downtown Seattle to Queen Anne Hill, Fremont and Ballard, as well as east to Capital Hill and Lake Washington. The system allowed distinct identities to arise for each neighborhood, yet all the while they were connected to downtown. With the relative ease of going back and forth to the downtown district, and as the population grew, the system encouraged further development. Housing became an increasing feature, and with it came small businesses. Further aiding the area was the arrival of the University of Washington after 1893, which suddenly brought a huge new "business" to the now appropriately named University District. No single entity played—and continues to play—such a large role in the area as the UW.

The area continued to grow after both world wars, the Great Depression, and, by the 1950s, the post-war boom. The freeway that split Wallingford from the University District was the first major blow to the area, putting financial interests above those of the neighborhood. By this period, the District had become a unique shopping area, for many a smaller yet still a major destination compared to downtown. When the Continental opened in 1968, the District was going through its biggest transformation as an oasis of the hippie movement.

It was, for many, a liberating period. Drugs, rebellion, even a kind of mild anarchy seemed to rule the area. I was too young when we took over the Conti in 1974 to understand the significance of this (teenagers rarely appreciate the historical significance of the time they live through), but only later in many conversations did this become known to me. By 1980 the hippie movement, such as it was, had died down and been replaced by homeless youth, who in time came to be pejoratively known as "Ave Rats." Social agencies in the area catered to this emerging population, yet at the same time, in doing so, in one of those paradoxes of life, they may have indirectly given agency to their presence in the area. At times it seemed to everyone in the area that this was the Ave Rats' territory; in a sense, they had taken over and the rest of us had to acknowledge their existence, whether we agreed with their lifestyle or not. It certainly made many of think about how much tolerance should be extended to others different from us, and at which point were we encouraging anti-social behavior. I could ask myself, what would Jesus do in such circumstances? He would do more than I ever imagined myself doing for them. I was torn; on the one hand I admired the Ave Rats for their apparent confidence and willingness to stick their noses at conventional society (something I could never do), while on the other their presence made life hell for the family operation. Many Ave Rats were involved in drug dealing. The drug dealing of the hippies was now replaced by a much more professional and aggressive operation—or so it seemed—that created challenges for local businesses. This drug dealing catered to the student population that lived or congregated in the area. They mixed in with regular shoppers and there seemed to have been a peaceful co-existence between the two. In general, the 1980s were popular years for the Ave.

Then came the beginning of the slide. The Ave's businesses had

For many, the first person seen when stepping inside the restaurant was Helen Lagos, and thus she even got her own menu dish: Helen's Pita.

become known for their longevity and quirkiness. Carter's Delicatessen, Porter & Jensen Jewelry, Nordstrom (later Place Two), the University Bookstore, and University Seafood and Poultry were just some of the well-known destination points in the District. The Continental was added to the list. Despite the opening of Costa's in the early 1980s, and the direct competition that this provided, the Conti managed to hold its own and even thrive. But in 1988 came the shocking announcement that the University Heights School would be closing. I was part of the effort to turn it into a community center (suggesting the name University Heights Center for the Community), but no one mistook this to be anything but a salvage operation. With the school closing, families would be forced to take their kids to other schools and in many cases to simply move out of the area. Fewer families seemed to appear on the Ave after this catastrophic event.

One of my earliest memories of the Ave from the 1970s was the special hours on Thursday evening when many shops on the Ave were open until 9 or so. This brought waves of people parading up and down the Ave, many pushing strollers, and turning the street into a weekly festival of shopping, eating, caféing, and simply hanging out. When the school closed, this wave ceased. Today, it has disappeared completely.

By the time I moved back to Seattle in 1989, the District seemed weak and tired. Competition with the ever-expanding Northgate and University malls brought further commercial decline as more and more mainstay operations either moved or simply closed. Distinct small businesses like Europa Europa, a clothing store (where I worked briefly), would leave and never be replaced. The multi-dimensional retail area was losing its verve and panache, replaced by chain stores with little character and distinction (including the McDonald's that replaced the beloved Carter's). The repaving of the Ave between 2002 and 2004 was an attempt to beautify the District, but in time the clean sidewalks turned brown and at times even bloody, with gangs fighting for turf, and in one instance, which I witnessed, the aftermath of a gang shooting.

Somehow the Conti managed to survive the changes. It became a mainstay, much like the Blue Moon, the Grand Illusion, Bulldog News, Allegro and other small businesses. It was still an artistically vibrant area, with many movie theaters and coffee houses and increasingly ethnic restaurants. What I had missed living in Los Angeles was the more human scale of Seattle's businesses. Los Angeles preferred bigness and power in its arts, whereas Seattle always felt small and more intimate. I loved going to the Seven Gables Theater and the Grand Illusion to watch movies, the Allegro coffeehouse for tea, and the Bulldog for newspapers and magazines. These quaint places reminded me of Europe, as places that connected to our souls, not just our pocketbooks. Not that LA was completely devoid of such places (the Old World could be counted as one), but Seattle seemed to have them in spades. Why this is the case remains a mystery for me. Is it the weather? Its liberal, progressive traditions? The arts always seemed to me to be muted in Seattle (unlike Los Angeles), but a more than adequate substitute could be found in the many glorious small businesses that became cultural icons for the city.

Yet, these places would in time come under pressure, and the pandemic proved destructive—with shortened business hours, greatly reduced foot traffic and an epic struggle to stay relevant while most of us stayed at home. Changing habits and demographics, new cultural changes and shifts to online purchases in the past two decades meant the European-styled places could not always compete effectively. They also reveal a sad new direction in the evolving history of Seattle: what was distinctive about the city seemed to matter less to the new generations or to those new residents moving in. Nothing exemplified this spirit more than the slow death of movie houses to Netflix and other video streaming services.

Movie theaters were one of the few instances when total strangers gathered in temporary community to remind us of our human bonds, however fleeting. Human beings once hungered for such places. We delude ourselves thinking that such communal spaces don't matter in the digital era; they actually matter more. There's nothing wrong with video streaming; we watch movies at home, too. But as a society we should try harder to pass the pleasure of live theater and movie houses to younger generations. We should pass on the pleasure of being in the company of audiences as a reminder that we're not automatons floating in a vast ocean of anonymity but part of the web of human existence. The Seven Gables Theater suffered from changing viewing habits, closing in summer 2020. When a fire destroyed it in early 2021, not just a great bijou had passed, but so had the memory that it once produced many memories for those lucky enough to attend a screening there. If anything, its existence was, for many of its fans, like me, a reminder that cultural institutions like a movie theater contribute to our daily sanity.

While LA would forever remain in my heart, Seattle was my home. But what I had come back to was a place that had fallen on hard times. The Conti, like many other businesses on the Ave, struggled to reach a new generation of customers that had less patience and even less admiration for iconic places like it. They wanted to be served, and whether it was a chain like Starbucks or a homegrown jewel like Allegro or Bulldog mattered very little to them. It was an emerging new mentality among this cohort of students that was more utilitarian and capitalist, and less spiritual and even cultural. While I did not fully appreciate the hippie movement of the 1970s, I did note its sense of experimentation and freedom to try new things. Later in my life I came to regard the seventies as a blessed decade, not from an economic standpoint (it was a disaster financially), but as a time when America's soul was exposed and a choice made as to where it would head—towards a more diverse, multifarious, integrated and democratic society or one that emphasized a growing militarization, corporatization, and economic stratification. With the election of Ronald Reagan, the country made its choice—opting for corporatization over democracy. We are the children of that decision today.

What that means is that the value of a place like the Conti slowly began to wane. I can celebrate its life-sustaining importance to the community (in later pages), but this importance diminished in value as a

Always in the mind of customers, the image that stands out the most: Helen Lagos perpetually on her feet, walking, serving, soothing, directing, smiling. She was infectious.

new ethos swept the land. Even liberal, progressive, trendy Seattle was not immune to the cultural forces swirling around it. One by one, the Contis of Seattle began to slowly fade away. And not just in Seattle, but around the country. It seemed never a month went by, for example, when the *New York Times* did not lament another neighborhood place shuttering in Manhattan.

Idealism had given way to a cultural toughness. I recalled a talk that movie star Robert Redford gave at Yale in the early 1980s that captured the same feeling, that society had taken a sharp turn away from the spirit of the tolerance and understanding and towards a competitive spirit instead. For an immigrant like me, America always carried with it a special dimension as a land that did not obey the laws of tradition and cemented social relations, but somehow found a way to promote newness, innovation, even the unrealistic. This spirit imbued our nation with a sense that it was indeed a special place, full of wonder and possibility, and that with a little bit of luck, achievement was possible, even likely. America had its deep-seated problems, but the ability to imagine a better future was not one of them. Few other countries in the world have that; most simply focus on survival as the overarching philosophy to life. America thrived.

Somehow the Conti became an oasis where the idealism still lived,

It was not a big kitchen; in fact, it was rather cramped. Yet, miracles came out of it in consistently great food. Here, an unidentified cook puts the final touches on one such dish.

and I think for many customers it became an attraction. There was no overt political discussion about it, just the feeling that—and perhaps it was the warmth that the family exuded to customers—a weary heart could find some solace and comfort at the Conti. We didn't have the best food in the world, or the best-designed restaurant—what we offered customers was a chance to take a break from a dog-eat-dog world, rest in the light (and with a skylight, literally) of care and regard. No one was turned away: Even homeless folks got a cup of coffee and a cookie.

In those early days after coming back from LA, I wondered how long the restaurant would survive in the new cultural environment. How long before it became an anachronism and out of date? Society never stops, and either folks go along for the ride or they get off. The Conti plugged along but for how long? It was doing well enough, and the 1990s turned out to be a decent decade. It had found its rhythm and had its loyal fan club. Sunday mornings were particularly busy.

When I came back from California, in some regards I was a different person, less withdrawn and more willing to speak my mind. I had few outlets before, but I now found new ones in Seattle. I began to write op-ed pieces for the *Seattle Times*, thanks to columnist John Hamer, and I also decided to make my own feature-length movie. My first op-ed was on my Greek American identity; thereafter they became more topical and even political. One caused controversy, and it involved my mother and the restaurant. An odd feature of the restaurant was a public telephone in the dining room just inside the entrance. How it got there and why are mysteries, but it was inherited when my father bought into the restaurant. It probably provided a small amount of income and added to the "community" feel of the restaurant. Occasionally, non-customers marched into the restaurant to use the phone.

One particular afternoon, as it happened, during a very busy lunch period one of the so-called "Ave Rats" (homeless youth) came in to use the phone. He was screaming into the phone. Customers turned their heads. Finally, having had enough, my mother went up to him and asked him to stop yelling. He did not oblige. Then my mother returned and asked him to leave. He reacted by punching her in the arm before dashing out the door. Two things happened after that incident. My brother got rid of the phone, and I wrote an op-ed in the *Seattle Times* about it, lamenting the state of the Ave that encouraged "outlaw" behavior in the young. Many local leaders that read the piece were upset, and one wrote a letter back indicating how wonderful the Ave was. About two weeks later, I happened to be walking down the Ave heading towards the University when I got behind two Seattle police officers who at that exact moment were discussing my op-ed. One lamented to the other that the only reason they were walking the Ave (and not attending to other duties) was because of the "asshole" (his exact word) that wrote in the *Times*. I did not have the courage to present myself as the asshole that had done it. I regret not doing it; it would have been at the least an interesting conversation.

I also decided to make a movie, a project I should have accomplished in Los Angeles but did not. It certainly stemmed from a creative desire to express myself, but also because I found myself stuck in the endless loop of working at the restaurant without purpose or direction. Even the occasional stint running food booths at local food festivals (the U–District Street Fair frequently, the Bite of Seattle regularly, once at Folklife) had little actual fulfillment for me.

The movie was, in the main, an act of desperation. It was a throw of the dice that fundamentally changed my life. It also revealed the limits of creativity. The world of restaurants and moviemaking are entirely different, yet they share some interesting characteristics. Both involve many people working on often tedious tasks, under conditions of long, physically-demanding hours, to produce a product which does not have a short shelf-life (for movies this was before YouTube). The similarities are particularly acute between the food booths that I ran (initially with a partner, then eventually on my own) and the movie I helped to make, *American Messiah*.

Food-boothing was one activity that intrigued me upon my return to Seattle. The Conti food both was started by a Greek American employee when the Bite of Seattle first began in 1982 at Green Lake. For three days, Seattleites enjoyed the ability to sample a variety of food, often reasonably priced in a park-like setting. Founded by Al Silverman, who got the idea from a similar festival in Chicago, the Bite took off and now is a main staple of the city's cultural scene.

When I returned in 1989, the Bite took place at Seattle Center, where it remains. I thought it might be fun and perhaps I could pick up a date or two. It failed on both counts. Preparations for the event for us began a few months prior to when it was held in mid–July, and when it arrived, we underwent three days of intensity that reminded me of the old days with Carol in the old kitchen—all under the watchful eyes of customers who witnessed our work. I worked hard and fast leading the assembly line. Then it took a month to recover from the insanity, only to do it again next year. When the employee left the Conti to pursue an actual career, it was left up to me to continue it. I did for some years before finally giving up.

Food-boothing gave me the confidence and wherewithal to make a feature-length movie. The restaurant was key to the enterprise. Not only would shooting take place there, but so would the entire operation be run from the Conti. Meetings were held there, and that's where I also held discussions with the personnel on the film. The idea for the film had been with me for some time; it had come to me in Los Angeles in the mid-eighties, and it did so as a title—*American Messiah*. Why and how to this day I do not know, but it was not the first time I had thought of a movie first as a title. Great, there was a title, but what about a story? That took far longer and a great deal of mental preparation (the myth that creativity is somehow a "divine" process of pure mental exploration is just that; in my life I have found creativity to be hard, difficult, and tedious work).

Over time, I came to see a resemblance between two powerful interests in my life: Christianity and filmmaking. I should perhaps be more specific—rather than Christianity, I mean to say the life of Jesus. From the time I was a young boy, going to church with my family fascinated me, in particular, hearing about Jesus and his exploits. There was something unusual about this man, born in a place that was not my village, who came to represent so many miracles, stories of decency and love, and a tragic ending. Who was this man and how had he captured my imagination? It says perhaps as much about religion as it does about my desire to learn what went on outside my immediate hamlet. Jesus came to be for me that force that beckoned me to learn about the greater world. But I knew there was more to his life than merely the icons in church and the retelling of his mission. I knew underneath the grand images in St. Nicholas Church in the village lay a world far richer and more soulful than I could imagine. It was a world beyond my imagination but one that Jesus sparked me to learn about. And, strangely, it came at my very first movie screening.

Taso the Movie Man brought his movies to the village every Friday. He came in an old white Chevy with a megaphone on the hood, driving around the village and announcing the film for the night. He put up a sign with black and white glossies and a small poster of the film. Interestingly, the black and white glossies sometimes remained the same even if the poster changed. I was around four when my parents one Friday afternoon announced that we would be going to see a movie that night, for me, the first time. So around nine in the evening, we got dressed in our Sunday best and my brother, my parents, and I strode to the village square and up the steps of one village café. There, set up on the roof over the café, were various chairs, benches in the front for kids, a bed sheet that flapped in the gentle summer breeze, and in the back, a projector attached to a generator.

I sat in the front with my older brother. When the movie (later I found out it was Charlton Heston's *Pony Express*) began, I found myself entranced as if taken into an intense, religious experience. It felt as if in that moment when the first images flickered on the screen, I had been inducted into some special place where the secrets of life had been revealed. It's strange to think this now, but at the time I simply had no reference to make sense of what transpired in front of my child eyes. From then on, I conflated movies with a religious, epiphanous experience. I still do.

So perhaps it was not so strange on my part to make my first major film a reflection of that early experience. The story that finally developed from the title dealt with a fictional movie crew making a film about the life of Jesus where one of the characters, a woman no less, playing a modern-day Jesus, starts to actually believe her role. It was also a commentary on the power and impact of Hollywood. I managed to write a few drafts of the script, but it was a good friend, Adam Gold, who finally produced a script that was the closest to my original vision. Then we set out to make it.

What today might cost a thousand dollars at the time (1992) became tens of thousands of dollars. I wanted a professional-looking film and it made sense to reduce the shooting time to something almost bizarre: four days. Most Hollywood features require several weeks if not months for shooting; we had to do it all in only a few days over Thanksgiving weekend. I reasoned that we might get lucky and professional cast and crew (without pay, except for the lead actors and the soundman) donate four days to us. They would not donate much more than that. To make life simpler for us, the script was written with a minimum of locations: the restaurant, the campus of the University of Washington, and an apartment in downtown Seattle. And we had a line producer, Virginia Lynn, a true and remarkable professional, helping us.

Our lead actor, John Keister, was a famous TV comedy star not only regionally, but thanks to Comedy Central, increasingly nationally as well. He was also a semi-regular customer of the Conti. I knew that if we could land him in the movie, it had a chance at getting distribution and attention. So, one day in the spring of 1992, I spotted him coming into the door of the Conti. Immediately I ran to the door and blocked him from entering unless he agreed to star in the movie. He agreed on the spot. Throughout the entire movie he was a complete professional, even if he did not get a dime for his efforts.

The night before the start of shooting, Thanksgiving eve, we invited all the cast and crew to come to the restaurant for a launch "party." We expected perhaps about twenty folks to show up; when nearly a hundred did, with my father getting nervous, it seemed that many had decided, without our prompting, to come and volunteer on the project. The next morning, at 6, we assembled for the start of shooting. Neither my mother nor father was particularly happy that we were filming in the Conti, least of all about the potential to wreak havoc on the restaurant. That we did not is a miracle. We had three film crews working simultaneously—the fictional film and two documentary crews filming the events on the set.

It became a strange project; perhaps the ultimate psychological

It was not just the family that made the restaurant the special, homey, charming place it was; the many servers contributed as well, some becoming friends of the family. Here Lisa St. George plies her trade with aplomb and cheer.

goal was to prove to my family that I could be a filmmaker, and not a restaurateur, that I had the vision and talent to make films as a career. And that might have been true had circumstances been a little different than how the project turned out. In the end, after burning through all my life savings and foolishly selling my Microsoft stock (it would later split at least eight times, before I stopped counting, which meant I could have been a millionaire had I kept it), I embarked on an adventure that was clearly above my head. The night we had our launch event at the restaurant was the same one when we discovered that no one had bothered to order the film stock. We had everything in place—the Panavision camera, the whole cast, and crew—but no film. We scrambled and managed to get some stock, with the help of the amazing Virginia, but it showed that luck was not on our side with this project.

While the shooting took only four days, it took five years to edit the final version of the film. A copy of the finished film was given to Scarecrow Video and a few hundred copies were sold through the mail, but otherwise, the film sank into oblivion. Once more I fell back on my work at the restaurant, aimless and restless now, wondering if a better future lay ahead for me. My mother claimed that the project was a way to clean out my system; for all my life she remembered I wanted to make a movie. Now I had, it did not go as planned, but at least I could check it off my bucket list.

The issue that stared me in the face, that I had trouble getting across to my parents, was that the Conti was increasingly an anachronism in the larger culture. My time at the Old World in Los Angeles taught me that society was changing, that more people were becoming interested in organic food and more nutritional, healthy food. By itself Greek cuisine is healthy, one of the healthiest ethnic cuisines in the world, but the creations we served at the Conti were a hybrid of Greek and American dishes that needed serious upgrading in my opinion. My parents did not share my vision. Arguments followed, sometimes over the most trivial matters—what should be the default choice of bread for the toast served with omelet and egg dishes? It had always been white bread, but I suggested we make it whole wheat. What about instead of deep-frying our Greek fries, we boiled them then warmed them up on the grill when serving them? What about serving brown rice instead of white, and preparing it without Crisco, but with something healthier? And so forth.

The battles increased in intensity and frequency; some even got ugly. My father stopped speaking to me for months at a time or, on one occasion, for three years. With the help of my brother and mother, I won a battle or two. The toast was changed to wheat bread, and we tried different oils in the deep fryer to make the fries healthier. But most of what I suggested fell on deaf ears. Curiously, though, some years after these battles, I was astounded to hear my father announce that he was going to change the "faki" (lentil) soup to a vegetarian version, removing the beef base that he always had put in it. He experimented for a while and came up with a recipe that to this day is the best lentil soup I have ever had.

The episode showed me that I had no real future in the restaurant business, at least, not at the Conti. I know my father had always spoken about my brother and me taking over the business on our own someday, but I realized that my ideas would not always be accepted. I was a "reformer," always looking to make something better and different. However, there is also another side to this issue. As smart and clever as I might have been at the time, I failed to realize that a restaurant is more than merely the food it produces. If people liked Greek fries as they were, then perhaps I needed to reflect on that as opposed to changing how they were cooked to improve their nutritional value. Maybe they came to the restaurant because they were making choices about what to put into their mouths.

It was becoming obvious that I wanted to convert the Conti into the Old World. It was not to be. When I harassed my father to remove the old spinning sign outside the restaurant that had become a symbol of the operation to a simple, but ultimately less distinct, blue awning, I had dealt a blow to history for the sake of change. I still remember the day the owner of the sign (we "rented" the sign from him, we could not own it) came to the restaurant to try to understand why my father wanted it down. My father did not want it down, I did, but for some reason he went along with the scheme. The well-dressed man was disappointed, but he took it well.

It was a minor victory for me; I think my father acceded to my request that we replace the sign out of a desire to give my brother and I more authority to smooth the transition to us taking over the place from him. In my heart, though, I knew it would never take place. I simply had bigger dreams to cultivate; owning a restaurant with my brother was not part of this. Okay, so what were those dreams now, since clearly they would not involve movies?

My grandmother, during my summer visits back to Greece in the 1990s, always considered me to be the Prodigal Son. I went to Los Angeles to make it, squandered what little money I had and my precious

71

time, yet returned to Seattle wiser for it, but still unable or unwilling to seriously get involved with the family business. I had a strong, psychic resistance to taking over the restaurant. Had I ever bothered to reflect deeply about this, I might have realized it was due to fear—an inability to believe that I had the tools and stamina to be in charge of a business. I just never thought I was up to the challenge of running a small business, with nearly twenty-five employees, a place known well and wide in the community, with a loyal and devoted customer base. It was simple fear that prevented me from taking over the Conti.

The only element that I could see, a myth I kept repeating to myself over and over, was that the restaurant business sucked up my life and my dreams and gave little back. This was patently untrue, but it was a way to avoid the reality of not facing my fears. Like any business or profession, it has its dark, less savory side: long hours, surly customers, disabled machines, rising rents, plugged toilets are just a few that come to mind. But there was another side to the business as well: the one that fed comfort food to hundreds of folks every day, brought smiles to sad faces, helped reunite old friends and even past enemies, brought people together into a sense of community, was a rest stop in a weary, fast-paced world, kept alive the idea that a neighborhood place really matters in the world and, of course, fed many a hungry belly. I simply did not understand, or could not and would not understand, that the Conti was more than a restaurant or a business, but a community institution that served an important, deeply social purpose for the neighborhood. Such wisdom came later on and from an unusual source.

CHAPTER FIVE

Restaurants as Community Centers

The drill was always the same. At exactly 2:30 each morning, I heard my mother step out of her bedroom, march down the short hallway and *plunk!*, drop her shoes onto the floor directly above my bed. It was the drop of her shoes every morning that always got my attention. She then marched to the bathroom whereupon a half-hour later she emerged, put on her shoes, grabbed her car keys and headed for the garage. A moment later, the engine of her car revved up, the garage door opened, and she was on her way for the twenty-minute drive from Edmonds to the University District. Monday through Monday, this was the routine. No days off, except for Thanksgiving, Christmas, and New Year's. Once, when Greek Easter and Catholic Easter fell on the same Sunday, my father closed the restaurant, much to the consternation of our regulars.

My father woke up between 5:30 and 6 a.m., by which time I was also awake and dressed, and we together followed my mother to the Conti. The tediousness of this day after blessed day had its own aura about it. We had become workhorses, my parents especially, my brother certainly, and I sporadically, and the toll this took on us took years to recognize. There were simply no moments to rest, to take a break (I did, frequently, leave for summer trips to Greece), or to enjoy life. My mother ended her shift at around three in the afternoon; she then drove home, bathed, watched the TV news, and by 7 was in bed. Sometimes, if there was a special event to attend at church, she might go to bed at 9 or 10. But no matter what time she slept, at 2:30 the next morning she was awake.

I knew her routine because for a short while when I started graduate school in 1997, I drove with her to help her set up the restaurant. This was the drill there:

- Arrive at the restaurant a little before 3 a.m., turn on all the lights
- Prep the kitchen by stocking the soups (lentil and avgolemono), the rice, the dolmathes, and the deep fryer
- Restock the bread supply if necessary
- Mop the entire floor in the pastry area, the bathrooms, the wait station, and kitchen
- Make sure the dishwashing machine is clean and tidy
- Check for any evidence of cockroaches and spray if necessary
- Turn on the hood system above the kitchen grills
- Clean the dishwashing area in the wait station
- Make sure that all the tables have cups and silverware
- Restock the pastry area with cookies and sweets as needed
- Get a newspaper for our customers to read
- Make sure all the machines (the oven, the fridges, etc.) are functional
- Clean up any human excrement left by the Ave Rats on the front door
- Turn on the heating system, especially in winter (when we arrived in the restaurant, the system was off, and it was freezing inside; yet we still had to prep the place until the heating system warmed it up)
- Restock the espresso machine with beans
- Make sure all the cups are clean; often the dishwasher from the previous night would not clean the cups properly, and we had to rectify this to save us the embarrassment of serving a "clean" coffee cup that was soiled to a customer
- Complete all these tasks and by 6 a.m. be ready to open the doors, even if the place was not officially open until 7 a.m.

I helped her prep the kitchen, but then left to go to my little office on campus to prepare for my graduate studies or be a teaching assistant in a class.

When my mother took a couple of weeks off to visit her mother in Greece, I became "Helen." It was not something that I looked forward to, and after doing many stints of this, it began to grate on me severely. In my thirties and forties, I resented mopping the floor at 3:30 in the morning. I did not feel this was what God or the universe had put me on this earth to do. In time this resentment overwhelmed me and distorted my view of reality. Once more, I was faced with the dilemma that haunted me when I first worked as a cook at the Conti—was this the final destiny and meaning of my life? It seemed however much I ran away from the restaurant, I was right back there.

I had become a utility man for the Conti. Whenever any member of my family was absent (rarely for my father), I filled in. I became "Helen" and "Demetre." Each demanded different sleeping schedules, and it was always hard to adjust. The most difficult was for my mother's shift; I had difficulty going to sleep early, so when I woke up at 2:30 as she did, I was not fully awake, and the rest of the day was painful. At least my brother's schedule—arrive at restaurant at 11 a.m. and leave at 11 p.m.—was more "natural."

I did this while maintaining a full class and teaching schedule at the university. Yet, I felt compelled to help the family and to assist my mother in her opening duties. For a brief time, I slept only four hours a night as I woke up at the same time as my mother, assisted her in prepping the kitchen, went to campus, played my role there, and returned to go home with my father around 9:30 p.m. each weekday night. I recall once saying this to a student in a statistics class. "Four hours?!" he regarded me, surprised. "Yup, that's all I get every night," I boasted. "Man, that's a luxury. I get three hours of sleep a night!" He was in the military attending school. I never again blurted to anyone else about my sleeping schedule.

What kept me going? Why did the family endure this physical regime?

There were many psychic rewards. Physical endurance aside, there was a strange comfort in the regularity of shifts. We knew what each day looked like, and even when surprises came—when the main baking oven broke; when a toilet was plugged and leaked; when rain flooded the back of the restaurant; when thieves broke through the skylight and lowered themselves into the dining area, cleaning out the cash registers; when someone had thrown a rock into one of the front windows; when a customer broke his tooth eating a souvlaki and all the other emergencies—the routine was set into stone and could not be altered. Our life was regulated by it, even as it required so much from our bodies, hearts, and minds to fulfill.

It was done because that was the way of living since our village days. The same force of will was evident then, too, in the hours spent tilling and maintaining our small farm plots and various orchards. I can still recall vividly being a small child on our wheat farm, and the back-breaking effort to cuts the blades, gather them onto a pile, then in the old-fashioned way of separating the stalk from the chaff, have our horse stomp around it, going in circles for hours at a time. Then with shovels we threw the stalks in the air to make sure we only had the kernels. This lasted hours. All around us other farmers did the same.

Yet, at the end of our labors, when the farming season was over, our family gathered with others in the area, and we held an impromptu picnic. If there was a single act of village life that I came to treasure, it was that at the end of hard work there was always a celebration, a moment of cheerful pride for the work done. We had no equivalent in the restaurant. If it became a grind and a toll on our bodies, it was because there was no celebration at the end of the day to let us know that we had done our hard work with pride and dignity. It was just going home and repeating the same acts the next day. And this went on for nearly forty years.

It is easy to hold the village up as a model of behavior, but parts of village life were less savory. The infighting, the petty clashes, the

4549 University Way N.E.
Seattle, Washington
632-4700

The to-go menu helped bring in new customers, or ones not familiar with the operation. The menu changed considerably over the years, although some mainstays—souvlaki and eggs, gyros, etc.— remained the same.

76

political battles that stewed behind the cheerful bonhomie were clearly there, but yet residents also knew that hard labor had to be met with celebration, that there are psychic rewards to life beyond money and status, and that we humans need to break our routines with a small festival. Since there was no equivalent at the restaurant, my parents (and to some degree my brother) found solace in the relationships we built with customers.

I do not believe that the Harvard Business School recommends that restaurateurs build relationships with their customers. If anything, the opposite is likely promoted. But we violated this rule because we needed to. My father had his own mini celebration at the end of each workday. Like he did in the village, when his labor was done for the day, he cleaned himself up, changed into clean clothes, and went out to the front to sit at the "family table." There gathered a special coterie of regulars that shared stories, occasionally argued politically, and otherwise replicated for my father what he had done in the village.

Even during those initial summers when I was his assistant, I followed my father's routine and joined him at the family table. It brought me out of the womb of the kitchen, I could people watch, and it provided me with social contact. If there is anything I miss about the Conti, it is those gatherings. We shared news, both good and bad, we laughed, we told stories, we enjoyed each other's humanity. Psychic rewards.

Do all Greek restaurants have such a table? In my travels to Greece, I notice that many do. I believe this is not so often the case in the United States; in that sense, we may have been an anomaly. But people came to treasure this aspect of the Conti, and to this day the groups that met there still do at other places. I understood why we are social animals.

The value of community revealed itself.

In 1997, I decided (well, my brother actually recommended it) to attend graduate school. By this time, *American Messiah* had gone nowhere (I did get a phone call from an organizer for the Cannes Film Festival who requested to see the film; I had to tell him that we ran out of money and did not finish putting together the film print) and yet another relationship breakup had thrown me into a deep funk. My family did not like seeing me depressed, and all of us remembered how much I loved books as a child. My friend Janet, who I had met when I volunteered to write for her small magazine *Simple Living*, lent me books from her self-help library. She had more than sixty books in her small collection. I read them all. And I was starting from the beginning again when I realized how much I had devoured them. Perhaps I could put the same energy towards obtaining my graduate degree. So, with the help of a customer who taught at the university, I applied. To my surprise, I was accepted. That, too, was another benefit of the Conti—the friendships with customers that directly led me towards important new steps in my life.

So that autumn, 1997, I found myself back in school at a time when my own mental energy was sapped and all I could think about was the former relationship. The "monkey mind," as Buddhists call it, had taken over, and I could think of nothing else. So, while still managing a few shifts at the restaurant, I became a student again.

Graduate school presented its own rewards and challenges, yet with the proximity of the restaurant, soon I came to love blending the two worlds, despite the conflicts that often came with this task. There were times when I needed to be at school, but during a busy lunch rush, I could not leave my mother alone to tend to the crowded dining area. So, I stayed to help, making my professors and advisors wonder about my commitment to my studies.

I now was a communications scholar. A new world opened up before me, the one about ideas and concepts and research. It was a world that I had never really known before—academia. Like Hollywood, it was its own separate world, with its own rituals, nuances, power struggles, and politicking. But yet there were also discussions about ideas that we could reflect on, a world-class library where I could pursue just about any subject, and the feeling that I had stepped into a special, protected sanctuary. In time I realized the university was my version of the Greek village that I always missed.

In the summer of 2003, I returned to the village to conduct my dissertation research. This was a big step for me. I had begun my grad schooling as a part-time master's student, not sure if I would like it or not, and by the second quarter in I realized that I did and became a full-time student. By 1999 I had obtained my master's, and as I sat with my advisor one day, she asked me if I wanted to continue towards my Ph.D. I nodded and said, "Why not?" These days that step is a much more complicated and formal one; at the time, it was just a matter of moving my file from one metal cabinet to another. And with that I had become a Ph.D. student, as well as a teaching assistant which allowed me to earn a small income and not pay tuition.

Many of my colleagues knew that I went to school but also worked at the restaurant. I was one of the oldest students (the second oldest), but this did not bother me one bit. My colleagues were very accepting; a small group of us formed, and we met often at the Conti. I enjoyed teaching, I was good at it, it seems, even once being nominated for a Distinguished Teaching Award. And I met many nice, attractive, stable women that opened up new vistas for me.

The highlight was preparing for the "final exams." This involved choosing a topic, and then, with my selected committee of examiners (four in all), negotiating with each one a reading list from which each professor would then question me. I was not to know what the questions were, although in my preparatory discussion with each examiner, I had a rough idea what I would be asked. So, the summer of 2001 was spent reading and taking notes on 120 books and articles, mostly books. It was a pleasant summer; I arrived with my father in the morning, caught a nibble, then marched to my small office on campus to continue the reading. In the afternoons, I found myself sitting on one of the quad benches enjoying the scenery but continuing my preparations for the exam, scheduled for September 13, 2001.

On Tuesday, September 11, I was driving my dad's pick-up to the restaurant as we did each morning, the radio tuned into KUOW, the National Public Radio station in the area. It was sometime between 6:30 and 7 when we heard a strange report that at first I took for a scene from a movie. Traffic was bad on I-5 South that day, so I had taken the 85th Street exit and was heading down Roosevelt towards the U–District when the report came on. There was screaming and shouting; something tragic was unfolding in Manhattan. By the time we arrived at the restaurant, where my mother always had the radio tuned to KPLU, another NPR station, we knew something shocking had happened. But I had to go to the university to continue my work, and so I tried to block the news from my mind.

When I got to the communications building, TV sets were on, and images of a plane smashing into one of the Twin Towers were being shown. As it happened, at that moment, my advisor and chair of my final exam committee walked in as I stood mesmerized by the images. She asked me if I wanted to continue with my exam scheduled to take place in two days' time. I thought about it for a moment and decided I could not postpone it, so in that moment, I had to return to focusing on my reading and put aside the tragedies of 9/11. Only some time later, after the exams, could I go back and relive what had happened on that tragic day.

The exam was a two-day affair that involved me being locked in a small office with only a desk and a computer and answering the

The operation was run from a tiny office at the end of a squeezed hallway. There was no room to breathe or move, yet it was made to work.

questions of my four examining professors. I could carry a notebook with me, but no paper or anything else to remind me of the readings. Whatever notes I had about the readings I had to carry them in my head, which I did, memorizing the main ideas of the 120 books and articles (as well as the author and the year the books were published). I would be in the room from eight until five, with a one-hour lunch break at noon. And this was repeated the next day, Friday.

This first day I arrived with my father, and after a really good breakfast and carrying the pillow that was recommended for me to making sitting more comfortable, I marched to campus. I had my temporary office in another building, so I went there to collect my head before starting the exam. I had slept well the previous night. So, at about a quarter to eight, it was time for me to find Carol, the administrator in the department, who oversaw my examination. As I walked from Raitt Hall to the communications building on the path along the art and music halls, I was struck by a piece of paper on the ground. It was about the size of a business card, and on it was a swastika. It was a stunning sight. I turned the card over and saw that it belonged to some political organization.

What shocked me most was to see this symbol, at that moment, in America. I didn't know if it had anything to do with 9/11, but suddenly I felt a river of emotions from knowing how my grandparents had suffered in the village during World War II when the Nazis swept through Greece (my father's parents were both killed) rising inside me. In that moment, no matter how tired and anxious I was about the exam, I felt a blast of energy from anger that I would put into the exam. I took the piece of paper with me. When I met Carol and she frisked me to make sure I had no hidden notes, I went inside the empty room, placed the swastika paper against the computer, and began to answer the questions. I was exhausted by the second day, but later my advisor asked how I had done such a good job. It was the swastika that gave me the fortitude to do so.

With the exam over, it was time for the dissertation, and I had to choose a topic for it. However, I had to choose a topic for my dissertation. It had to be original work. I could not simply go to the library, read several books, and write a lengthy paper. I had to conduct original research. Choosing a topic proved to be difficult and time consuming. I had an opportunity to research a topic in political economy, but it proved to be too difficult. So, finally my advisor and I opted for a simple, "researchable" topic—regarding the diffusion of new communication (i.e., radio, telephone, television, etc.) technologies in rural Greece. And best of all, I could go back to my village and conduct the research there. Easy. It turned out to be one of the most difficult experiences of my life, difficult in the sense that research is never easy or straightforward.

Yet it was also became illuminating. My interviewees revealed to me the importance of the village cafés in spreading the arrival of new communication technologies. Up to that point, my knowledge and awareness of community was nil. I had been excited to read about "social capital," or the ability of human beings to interact in collaborative, sharing, caring ways, but it never extended to the concept of community. The concept itself is generic, bland, and defies description. What exactly is community? Are members of a neighborhood disposed towards community? Are people traveling together in an airplane or watching a movie in a theater community?

In the case of village cafés, they were the first to introduce technologies into the communities. This seems simple enough, but when I began to break it down, I realized that there was more to it than simply introducing, say, the telephone or TV to villagers. That in itself is not noteworthy. What it revolves around is anxiety. Diffusion of innovation theory (yes, there is such a theory, and, yes, it involves how technologies, ideas, awareness, etc., spread out and in the general population or in a given community) reveals that any new product or idea causes "anxiety" (both good and bad) in individuals. Instinctively, we recoil at the thought of something new—a relic from our past hundreds of thousands of years ago when our species, like most animals on earth, had to be aware of changes in the environment (a marauding lion, an earthquake, a coming storm, etc.) to stay alive. So, we are biologically attuned to our environments and any slight change to it. When new products or ideas are introduced, these represent changes to our environments. How do we deal with them?

In the case of villagers, who suddenly were introduced to an array of communication gizmos in the twentieth century, they were overwhelmed. Because these innovations were first witnessed in the familiar and trusted village café, they seemed less threatening and even could be exciting. The village café acted as an anxiety reducer in the community. People's opinions of these products I discovered in my interviews were very positive. But when the village café as a social institution began to die with the spread of TV in the community, when villagers stopped going to the *kafenion* in the evening after work, new communication technologies ceased being introduced there. So, for example, mobile telephones and computers (a natural addition to a café) were not introduced in the *kafenia*, and many individuals had remarkably negative associations with both products (they caused cancer, were too complicated to operate, and so on).

Suddenly I was placed front and center in understanding what makes a community work. Institutions like the village café transcended their business mandates and became important social glues. When I returned from my trip to Greece, I had a newfound appreciation for the Conti. It was simply a *kafeneion* planted in the middle of a busy Seattle neighborhood. Its value was not that it provided food and a place to grab coffee and a dessert, but it was a hub, a gathering place, a rest stop between home and work, or the so-called "third place."

Why hadn't I seen this before?

Because it never mattered to me before. The more I learned about such regenerative community, the more I understood its importance to a place. It literally could be any location; I read about a medical clinic in the Philippines that was an important and trusted community center and general stores in some rural parts of the U.S. that had taken on such an importance to its surrounding areas. This was true too for some cooperative grocery stores on the East Coast that did the same for their neighborhoods. These types of places were literally everywhere yet I had been blind to them.

It changed my conceptualization of the Conti. I could complain that

This card was made by a customer whose name is no longer known but who provided the kind of memory that is appreciated in a memoir.

as a business and career, it had little sway for me, yet, as for hundreds of our regular customers it had become, as my dissertation called it, a "mediating commons." It transcended its business practice to become a trusted, vital, important, and necessary salve for a community starved of authentic human contact. Many customers regarded our family as their "borrowed" family and returned there countless times to eat and join its lively, sharing, caring spirit.

My parents instinctively knew this but never shared it with me, or at least were not capable of articulating it in a way that I could understand. It's not a concept that we normally go around and discuss. The weather. Our jobs. Traffic. Our elected officials. But not community. It occupies the realm of psychic rewards that stands outside of our consciousness, even as it soothes and replenishes it.

For the first time in all my years being involved, directly or indirectly, in the operation, I grew to admire the place as more than a restaurant, but an oasis of humanity. I recall how my family never once in all the years that I ever observed ever turning down a request by a homeless person for something to eat or a cup of coffee. Even the bathroom we made available to those folks who lived on the street, despite the fact that they sometimes left messes behind. I don't know if it was our magnanimity, or simply an extension of what the Conti had become for the neighborhood: not just a business, but a social institution that cared about the community.

My dissertation was completed in 2004, and I received my doctor of philosophy degree the same year. It had been a long, difficult but rewarding period. I finally had my Ph.D., which would open doors for me. In less than ten years, we would no longer own the place, but at the time it seemed that the Conti would live forever. My brother and his family would take it over from my parents, and the social institution would continue.

But by June 2013, that would no longer be the case.

CHAPTER SIX

Must It Always
Involve Stereotypes?

We knew him as "Crazy Eddie," a derogatory name for a man who clearly had mental health issues but whose gentleness and childlike wonder moved all those he interacted with. He was a short, slight figure with unkempt hair and a friendly, bright smile that disarmed me. In the grand scheme of things, Eddie was a pitiful figure who was trampled by life and seemed to hang on to it by a thin thread. No single human being that I encountered at the restaurant ever matched the desire of this solitary, lonely, mentally-challenged figure to simply stay alive despite all the odds arrayed against him that made it as difficult and as vicious as possible. He was a figure that floated in and out of the restaurant, completely at random moments, disappearing as quickly as he appeared, a mythical figure in some way with few burdens except the biggest one of all—yearning to be part of this world, almost desperate to do so.

A nation is great by the ways it treats its least able and weakest citizens. Under such a mark, America has failed in her mission to protect the defenseless and disabled. There was simply no space for such an individual; he was not gainfully employed and could never be, yet he brought us as much joy and inspiration as anything our culture ever produced.

There are his stories.

Without his medication, he cut a forlorn, angry figure. Once, during a very busy lunch rush, he came in to use the bathroom. I happened to be there and noticed him coming in without greeting me, a dark cloud hanging over him. I watched him go to the bathroom, and as he did, he grabbed an empty glass from the dirty-dish tray and took it with him. I immediately notified my father. He rushed to the bathroom and opened the door. I was only a few feet away and witnessed the event.

Eddie had broken the glass and was trying to slash his wrist. My father looked at this and without breaking stride, blurted out, "Eddie, what're you doing? You can't do that now. Come back after the lunch rush!"

The pathetic figure gave him a look of equal parts shock and bewilderment, as if shaken from his sad reverie, and abruptly flew out of the bathroom and out the front door. Maybe my father's odd comment caught him off guard enough to make him stop and leave. When he came back a few months later as his usual beaming self, I knew that he was all right.

There was a time when he had not come to the restaurant for some months. I worried about him, fearing the worst. I asked other regulars if they had seen Eddie, but no one had. Eight months after the last sighting, he walked in on a bright summer afternoon. I jumped to my feet as if greeting a long lost relative, which, in a way, he was. Or perhaps the Prodigal Son.

I immediately prepared a feast for him. He clearly was not used to such treatment, and my mother (ever the financial hawk who counted every penny of expenditure) watched with a weary eye. As he devoured soup, bread, rice, coffee, cookies, and more soup, he told us his sad story of why he was absent all this time.

A block north of the restaurant is a Safeway supermarket. One day he was wandering around the parking lot, and, feeling tired, he climbed onto the back of a semi-truck. He must've have fallen asleep for, apparently, when the truck came to a stop many hours later, he found himself in Chicago. It took him eight months to find his way back to Seattle.

Everyone who heard this suddenly erupted into laughter, including me. Eddie was caught off guard by the impact of his story, and in a strange way it brought him comfort and pride. He was overwhelmed and soon left, perhaps unable to handle the impact his story had on others. I think he was even moved by it. That was part of community, too, part of the wonder and glory of the Conti.

The story became a legend around the family table.

Eddie knew my father by name. "Hey, George," he uttered when entering the restaurant. "Can I have a cookie and coffee?" He immediately got his chocolate butter cookie and coffee, and then he disappeared. I wonder where he is now, what he is doing, and how he is surviving. The longevity of street people is not high. Over the years we watched as one by one, homeless folks we knew and catered to with cookies and coffee died one by one. No mention in the *Seattle Times*, no lamentation by anyone over their loss, just the empty feeling knowing they died (or is it vanished?) without a trace. Such stories rarely receive media attention; the homeless die as invisible people.

I watched a parade of these folks wade through the garbage in the alley behind the restaurant. Usually the lid was locked for such

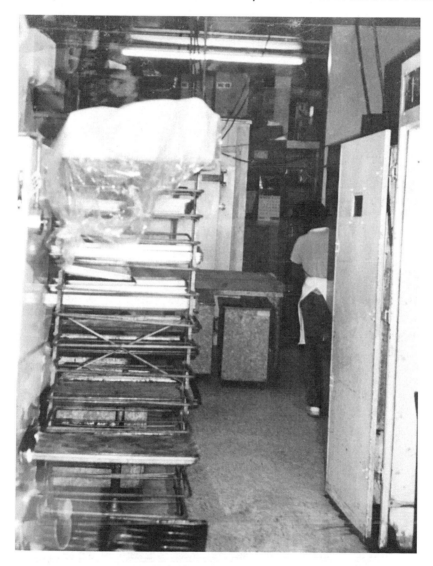

If the kitchen was cramped, imagine the prep kitchen, which squeezed far too many elements into a tight space. Lacking air conditioning, it melted all who worked in it during the summer months.

moments, or to avoid strangers throwing their garbage into ours. In Greece there were no homeless, certainly not in our village, and even in Athens they were rarely (until the economic crisis hit in 2010) seen. So, it was quite a shock to see so many folks living on the street, and it seemed the U–District was a particular magnet for them. I don't know how other restaurants treated them; my suspicion is not very well. I found this out indirectly when I briefly ran for Seattle City Council in 2014–15. As a stranger entering several Ave restaurants, I got very chilly receptions. Few, in fact, were even polite to me. I imagined what it must have been like for a homeless person to enter such a place and what a wonder it was for them to visit the Continental.

Over the years I learned to deal with my own stereotypes of the homeless. Whatever we assume in them (mental illness, drug or alcohol addiction) may have some basis of truth, but homeless is a general term that unfortunately has come to describe a category of human beings who truly defy description. One man in particular, who I still see around the District, is one of the most articulate and dignified human beings I have ever met. He frequently is seen carrying a big plastic bag over his shoulder (the bane of homeless life is that you must carry your stuff with you at all times to avoid theft; it's why so many such folks push overfilled carts) and often a bandana on his head. I offered him food and he often refused; money he accepted more frequently, but not always. He never smelled, so somehow he kept clean, and he never bothered or solicited anyone.

I have come to appreciate such folks as features of the neighborhood, and while others have been less charitable, leaving droppings at the front door that either my mother or I cleaned up consistently throughout the year, I cannot be angry about this for too long, especially knowing the harshness of their lives.

When asked during my run for Seattle City Council how we can solve homelessness, my response is yes, it can be done, but it requires the help of the entire community, was not just social workers and Good Samaritans, and funding from the city. Everyone in the community needs to pitch in. I don't know what impact my response had on folks (I am not sure they were happy with the answer I gave them), but I still feel that this is not just a municipal "problem." Homelessness confronts us all, and it will never be solved unless more people pitch in to help. It means collectively doing our bit to relieve the stigma and social exclusion of homelessness as a moral issue, not simply a social one.

On my return from Los Angeles, I confronted past demons of my place in the world. It seemed I struggled to find it and only when I began graduate school did a road that satisfied finally presented itself. I relaxed about the difficulty of my commitment to the restaurant. Graduate school was getting harder and harder with each passing year, and my time was limited. It became obvious to many and to me that it was no longer working out for me. I was in my forties by now, and it simply became harder and harder to survive on four hours of sleep at night. My body was feeling the toll this produced, and it left me vulnerable to sickness.

There were two instances I got sick that told me the restaurant environment was not for me. One was during the spraying to kill cockroaches. Every restaurant (and there are no exceptions) has to deal with this issue. Where there is food, the smell of food, any kind of grease and heat, there will be cockroaches. It's a given. How they are dealt with is a matter of choice for the owner or manager, but dealt with they must be, unless one wishes to see the entire operation overrun by them.

This is why my mother mopped the floor clean each day, from front to the back; it had to be cleaned in order to keep the cockroach population at bay. But there were times when the place had to be sprayed, usually the kitchen. In those instances, if I breathed the fumes, within days I was ill with a cold or flu. There was no exception. I should have worn a gas mask, but I never did. I had to ask my parents to tell me when they planned to spray so I could avoid the Conti that day.

The other instance came as a surprise to me during preparations. It came during preparations for the food festivals that I organized for the Conti in the 1990s. While planning began a few months prior to each event, it was about a week before the actual festival dates that preparations were made in earnest. Not only did we have to make dozens of large buckets of "tzatziki" (a dressing of yogurt, garlic, cucumber, and spices), but also the thousands of "souvlaki" or shish kebabs. This meant working with hundreds of pounds of beef, chicken, and gyro meat. The gyro meat came already sliced, so that was easy; the other meat had to be trimmed and then cut and then marinated in large rectangular plastic buckets. Such preparations took over the entire restaurant; finding storage space during those days was difficult.

I helped on the meat preparation, but I noticed that each time I completed the preparation, I got sick. This presented a serious problem when the opening day of the food festival came; I faced three of the most intense working days of my life, but I could barely stand on my feet. What was it about handling the meat that made me sick? It's true that I have a sensitive constitution and others did not react like I did, but it did raise the issue of whether chemicals in the meat (hormones and the like) were causing my illnesses. I never found out because I never told anyone or ever asked. I supposed if I Googled now I could solve the mystery, but the desire is not there.

This was perhaps the biggest reason why I decided to stop doing the food festivals and find another, more stable income producer. And it was not just getting sick that was a problem; relying on the capricious weather made life hell for us. When it rained, crowds fled, and we were left sitting on buckets of tzatziki lamenting what would happen to all the prepared foods. I was responsible for all the purchases, not the restaurant, so it was on my dime, and there were several times (particularly during the U–District Street Fair) where torrential rain destroyed business for those days.

As a community institution, we all had ways of contributing to the improvement of the Conti. My sister was the one that came up with the "platter" name that became a mainstay of the lunch menu. I pushed for better, more nutritious toasted bread to be served with breakfasts, and so forth. Yet, one contribution that I made came by accident. By the early 2000s, with my focus on completing my graduate work, I had less reason to battle my family over what I thought was a big improvement. It simply was not worth it anymore. So, I simply concentrated on my studies and left the restaurant to my family. It was perhaps my way of avoiding family conflict and all of us being on each other's good side.

As part of the family that owned the restaurant, of course, I had certain privileges. I could eat any time I wanted (which became part of my daily routine; arrive at the restaurant with my mother, then help her prep the kitchen, leave and return for lunch, where I often helping out if it were busy, and return for dinner at the end of the day). Over the years I experimented with making my own dishes; this was partly in reaction to eating the same dishes over and over again, but also because I am an experimenter.

I am a big fan of rice. One of my regrets was that my family could have served brown rice, cooked not with Crisco but butter, or simply better yet, steamed the Asian way. My father refused. One day, out of boredom, I decided to try something different. I am a big breakfast person, so this meal was always important for me. I took the omelet mix, threw some of it on the grill, and then sautéed some mushrooms that we used for the omelets. Then I put the cooked eggs and mushrooms on top of the heap of rice, and added feta cheese, oregano, and some olive oil. Delicious and filling. Customers began to ask me about the dish, so

I made it for them. They loved it and soon asked for it regularly. My parents decided to put it on the menu, "Taso's Breakfast." I joked that I was named after the breakfast, not the other way around. It became a huge hit, and I wonder if anyone has copied this at another restaurant. I hope they have; it remains one of my favorite dishes, and I would hate to know that it died out with the passing of the Conti.

I also came up with "Taso's Fruit Salad," but this was a seasonal dish (not something served in the winter, for example) that had less success. Why name the dishes after me? Lest it be thought that I was arrogant, the real reason was because I couldn't come up with a better name.

Lurking behind these innovations was the stark reality of tensions within the family. We could congratulate ourselves for the accomplishments made at the Conti—an immigrant family who arrived in the United States unable to speak English had in a few years managed to take over a popular restaurant and in the process become fully assimilated into the culture while continuing its success. My mother by now could read and write English, was a superb server, a steady guide, and a detailed-oriented manager. My father ran the kitchen with a firm but humane hand, and my brother took care of everything else with calmness, equanimity, and understanding. We had a very low turnover when it came to employees; our workers very much were treated as and became members of our family. And, above all, we were a neighborhood institution that was a second home to hundreds of regular customers.

If it is true that life gives with one hand but takes with the other, then the gifts were enormous but so were the sacrifices. Family life as I knew it, both in the village and then when we came to the United States, was one of independence and space. I would not and could not say we were a very tight-knit family; my earliest memory of this world was village life as my own backyard. Home was where eating, sleeping, washing, resting, etc., took place, but it did not define us. My father seemed to spend more time in the *kafenia* than at home. My mother had her circle of friends that visited her. My brother and I felt free to pursue our own interests and desires. For me that meant a variety of games, from kiting in the spring to climbing trees and trying to charm our next-door neighbor's daughter.

Life in a restaurant is like no other. There is the tremendous strain and intensity and long hours of constant, tedious work, and the madness when a rush suddenly hits (we have seen the place go from empty to packed in a matter of minutes) and life turned into an assembly line. If days are the markers by which we measure our lives, for restaurateurs, days are numbers to be checked off on a calendar. Tomorrow will be like today, with problems that we cannot foresee. But there will be problems and challenges, to be sure. We can't plan or predict what they will be.

It was being in a boxing ring every single day. And those days become weeks, months, seasons, years, and eventually decades. Escape? That is a dream that never came. I was the only one in the family who sought it and got it, with frequent trips to Europe and seven years living in Los Angeles, but it came with a reputation for being lazy. I would never be considered a reliable member of the family because I simply did my best to avoid the place as much as I could. Whenever I had any serious dream of taking it over, I pictured transforming it into something that it was never meant to be. My brother wanted to take over the restaurant from my father, but it seemed impossible to pry it from his hands. He had his own ideas of what the Conti could be, yet so did my father. And my mother. And at times even my sister. They were good plans for the most part, and no doubt they would have helped the place continue.

In the end, however, those plans were done in because we found no common understanding of our family and our relation to the Conti. We never quite understood what we had, and therefore, when it was finally gone, we were left with holes in our souls because we failed to appreciate the role the Conti played in our lives. The truth is that we spent too much time in the grind, rarely stepped back from it, and found no real assuring rhythm of how to deal with the tremendous stress of running the operation. We went from spending little time with one another to seeing each other for ten hours per day, 362 per year. We were glued to each other and this familiarity bred resentment. It had to; no family can withstand that kind of intense interaction and not feel frustration.

Could it have been avoided?

Unlikely, since we came to rely on each other to fulfill certain roles. Whenever my mother decided to visit her aging mother in Greece, I filled in. Likewise, my brother. My father never left. The Conti was his home in every sense of the word. The home in Edmonds merely held his clothes and allowed him to take showers. Nothing more. He became a barnacle permanently attached to the Conti. The two, in fact, became inseparable. He had no life outside of the restaurant. He didn't want one. Nothing could take him away from the place, on pain of death.

Even darkness needs daylight, if only to separate itself. When we took over the Conti, we left our independence behind. We became its slaves (not a word to be used lightly), more so than the physical dimensions of slavery are the mental ones; in time, I felt as if there were no world but the Conti. All of human history and the majesty of life was boiled down to a restaurant located at a specific point on a specific street in a specific town for the duration of eternity. It never seemed possible that life could or would exist outside of such confines. We were wedded and welded to the place, our identities emanated from the place, and therefore we were its face to the public. It was our master, when in reality a place is simply walls and a floor, a ceiling, furniture, equipment, supplies, doors, and lights. That's all it is. We breathe life into it, and we pull the plug on it. But you never knew that by watching us.

We became robots in the service of the restaurant. We had to do it, we felt, or the place would die. This was a fiction we told ourselves, perhaps to feel needed and a part of something greater than ourselves, but still nevertheless a fiction. I wondered if at times the Conti had not become its own mini religion, with its own set of rituals and incantations, or, alternatively, a giant monster that required the feeding of our time and energy.

A different approach might have worked better. Had we seen it for what it really was, it might have saved us from the sad ending. It didn't have to end the way it did. We have no one to blame but ourselves. But this is in retrospect. At the time it was more difficult to be reasonable and even rational. We had work to do, customers to serve, tables to bus, bathrooms to clean, food to cook, orders to make, etc. We knew our customers loved us and sought us out as rest stops in a sometimes cruel world, so we assumed we were being Good Samaritans. We gave of ourselves so others could continue their lives, even at our expense.

One of the biggest lessons I learned being a father is that my wife and I must first take care of ourselves before we take care of our daughter, for the same reason that on flights we are told to put the oxygen masks on ourselves before our children. And this was perhaps our biggest failing; we did not honor our own needs but put those of others—our customers—above our own. The price we paid was built-up resentment that ate away at us, slowly at first, and then in time with greater speed and ferocity.

No one really noticed this until the end, although we were intimately aware of the resentment it created. As much as we showed joviality and good cheer to our customers, we revealed anger and mistrust to each other. There was never a sense of clearing the air, because if we tried it might have led to still more tension, so we avoided any kind of open, honest communication. We were frozen in a weird zone of indifference and fallacious stability. We seemed the perfect family to the outside world when in fact we probably ceased to be a fully functioning one some time before my dad sold the Conti. We lived off the fumes of the past as a family unit; we coasted along on the merits of our ways from Greece, but in time these became stale and ineffective.

We stopped being a real family.

I regret that because it was not a pre-ordained conclusion. It could have been avoided. No one forced us to stop being an honest family. We made that choice, although perhaps less consciously than we might have suspected. And this lack of family spirit affected our physical energy. It is interesting how strong the body can be, but how weakly it reacts to a tired spirit. A hearty, determined spirit can make a tired body move, but not the other way around. Our spirit, which we inherited from a tiny, but in my mind paradisiacal, village in Greece had withered and finally vanished. We had no more to give to anyone because our tanks were empty. Selling the place was inevitable.

I had felt this about ten years before the end came, and I even uttered it to my mother, but she did not believe me. "We may lose this place," I said to her, exasperated one day, when the tension boiled over, but she hardly listened or even understood. I had that role in the family, too: the canary in the coal mine. Such canaries exist, but it takes special people to listen and to heed their warnings.

Since my parents retired, I have become very interested in management, if perhaps out of some psychic need to understand the circumstances behind our downfall. I read constantly of operations and even countries that fall to ruin because of mismanagement. Sports teams are particular favorites of mine; as I write this the champion in the English Premiere League (football, or soccer to us), Leicester City, faces relegation this season due to poor performance. How does a team go from being champion to nearly in last place the following season?

Somewhere along the line the team exhausted itself, and it ceased being a functioning unit. It stopped recognizing its real purpose and instead floated on its reputation, an always dangerous element. Reputations cannot substitute for character. But it's an easy trap to fall into because the hard path requires skill and dexterity. It means units having good communication skills and the temerity to never fall prey to routine. All our actions are special because in time we recognize that it's the only "thing" we produce—and eventually these actions will stop as we invariably come upon death. It wasn't really until towards the end that it dawned on me that hundreds of thousands of times over the course of nearly forty years folks trusted us to let us cook for them and to put our food into their bodies. What other ways do we let anything enter our bodies without knowing something about it? This trust is extraordinary; we were its beneficiaries, because that placed us in an exalted position. Imagine if our food gagged our customers. How long could the Conti be so sustained?

There is nothing routine about life. Yet, we forget that and turn it into the familiar because it is easier. To think otherwise requires effort, consciousness, deliberation. It's the intentional life. Our actions have consequences, so we make sure we are thoughtful in what we do. We take nothing for granted, because tomorrow all could vanish. Our nation can become weak and indifferent. We live off our past and treat the present as if it were the future. The present is the link between the past and the future, but it is also the one element we can consciously influence. But we otherwise regard it as simply one giant continuum; we are confronted by a constantly shifting array of different paths that we are free to choose from; they do not choose us unless we allow it. We can make a real difference in today when that power is carefully weighed in our minds. But it necessitates thinking clearly and honestly.

The Conti is now a dream, part of the ages, and no longer a force in our lives except its memories and what it represented for hundreds if not thousands of people. We became Leicester City, forever now wondering what might have been had we done things a bit differently. A bit more deliberately. A little more thoughtfully and carefully. We didn't appreciate what we had until it was too late.

George Lagos was a more relaxed figure as retirement beckoned. It was a sad day for others, but he needed rest and he looked forward to a lot of TV watching.

And now we live with this knowledge. True, we were aging, and our bodies creaked. If my father pulled the plug it was out of desperation—enough is enough. But it did not have to end as it did; another family might have taken over the Conti and continued its traditions. We could have found another "Lagos" family to continue this important neighborhood institution. We didn't. And that was part of the lack of deliberation as well. Perhaps no one believed my father when he announced he was ready to get out of the Conti. He had threatened this before. Listening is part of deliberation, too, to regard words as not just noise, but deeper reflections of thoughts.

For me, I had been aware of such a possibility for some time but stopped saying anything about it. If I did, the next question invariably was "Then why don't you take it over?" I didn't have the stomach, or the courage, to do so. At the time, it seemed beyond me. And so I kept my mouth shut. The train had long left the station, and who was I to stop it? And when my brother decided that it was no longer for him, the entire operation collapsed. He no longer carried the torch of the place, and at that moment I knew it was over.

The Conti would be no more.

CHAPTER SEVEN

Restaurants as Cultural Assimilators

Since I worked on the campus near the restaurant, it was hard to escape the many customers who either lived or worked near it that were very sad, angry, disappointed, or stunned by the loss of the Continental. And the onslaught came immediately. The news of its impending closure was widely known, and on the day before we transferred power to another family, the *Seattle Times* had a front-page story about it. I had an op-ed in the *Times* about it as well.

So, then, what happens when a restaurant is sold?

Besides the protestations of our closing came the question of how to keep the memory of the Conti alive. I had no real answer for the folks who were upset about the restaurant's loss, since I was equally as upset by its loss as they were. I lamented with them as much as they lamented with me. And so it went, and to some degree still does, although with each passing day the Conti recedes in the minds of its most ardent fans. The lamentation kept going at the time, so I wondered if there was a way to deal with it and keep the memory of the Conti alive. It came from an unexpected place.

For me, the legacy of the Conti that most stood out was that it had become my home. Not the physical one where I slept, but the one where I spent most of the day's hours. I slept at the house where I lived, but the rest of the time (including showering on campus) took place in the U–District. It was, in short, my authentic home. Home is an interesting word since it represents many ideas: a place where you are comfortable or familiar or where you have your legal residence. There are places in the world where a person is not required to live in a community to run for office there (perhaps most notably in England). In the United States, certainly in the state of Washington, there is a residency requirement for office seekers.

In 2013, voters in Seattle did something historic—they passed Charter Amendment 19 to change the City Council system from an all-district voting scheme to one where seven members of the nine had to be chosen from specific districts. The remaining two were selected at large as previously. The Fourth District was the U–District. For a brief time, I was involved in the campaign to support Charter 19; during a press conference, I was the one that appeared dashing in front of the camera fixing the sign that was falling from the speakers' table.

I saw the passage of the amendment as an opportunity for me to keep the memory of the Conti alive, and perhaps to also take advantage of its good name. I also felt I was qualified to run, since I knew the District well from working at the Conti. It was also my home.

In the same month that the amendment passed in the local election, my wife and I bought a home in a section of unincorporated Snohomish County. In a few months, she would be pregnant. A week after the baby was born, I announced my candidacy to represent the Fourth. A friend allowed me to rent a room in his house to establish my residency. Some years prior to this event I had begun a series of dialogues with a local political activist to whom I related my political interest. He encouraged me to run. After lengthy discussions with my wife, despite being a newly minted father (a "fossil dad" to be exact), I took the plunge. I was primarily motivated as not only someone who cared about the neighborhood but one who wanted to see it continue as a viable place for artists, students, faculty, workers, and families to live and work. I also was concerned about moves to "up-zone" the area and turn it into a second downtown with high office towers. I knew that once this took place, the flavor and uniqueness of this area, particularly its many ethnic restaurants, would come under pressure from higher rent. I continued my teaching at the university, despite now unleashing a campaign and still having to help take care of the baby at home.

Sleep suddenly became a privilege, not a right.

Motivation for this effort also came from my own academic interest in digital democracy and social justice. It is one matter to read and study politics; it is quite another to actually engage in it. It proved to be a fantastic but painful lesson. First of all, it is a cutthroat world, more so than I could have ever imagined. Even in progressive Seattle, the backstabbing that takes place in politics stung my naïve sensibilities and idealistic notions of the world. I wanted to engage in good debates over the future of the Fourth; instead, I faced social media whispering campaigns of being a "carpetbagger." It slid downhill from there.

Until April when I mercifully pulled the plug on the teetering campaign, I found myself swimming in open waters, under a vicious storm, with torrential rains and blistering winds. And I felt something tugging at my feet below. It was not a scene painted by Norman Rockwell. It was my induction into local politics and democracy. The Conti, of which I spoke about at every open-mike session I faced, became part of my stump speech, and I saw it caught a nerve with many voters. They knew the place, they remembered my family, they nodded at the need to keep such neighborhood places alive. This was the best part of the campaign. Finding a good campaign team was the opposite. I had strong support from my friend who offered me his house, and several businesses on the Ave also indicated their willingness to help me, but I was hamstrung by juggling three massive balls—working, running a political campaign, caring for a tiny baby—that were at cross purposes. My wife continued to work. It became, to quote from the movie *Zorba the Greek*, the "full catastrophe."

Yet, the campaign revealed to me the extent of the restaurant's legacy. I was constantly surprised by voters' enthusiasm when I brought up the Conti as an important part of why we had to save the neighborhood from sweeping zoning changes. The up-zoning would destroy the area as much as it would shift power away from neighborhoods and towards city hall. The up-zoning was simply a political means to consolidate power within the elites of downtown. Reasonably priced apartments in the area would immediately disappear, and those artists and workers who made the district their homes for decades would be replaced by expensive condominiums that had already swept in.

Growth should be managed carefully and judiciously, but, in the case of the district, it witnessed developers given carte blanche to transform a sleepy community into a bustling business district with little regard for the desires of residents who live and die there. Seattle was growing and bursting at the seams, but what made it special was being lost in the rush for development. Destroying the fabric of a neighborhood to "improve" it is not progress. In those few times I was able to get my voice heard, whether one-on-one with voters or shop owner or via the media, I explained the reasoning behind this. Most people listened, and it made sense to them. I explained that when land values rise precipitously, as was the case with the U–District, with expectations of coming high-rises, no longer does the community become a real neighborhood; instead, homeowners are turned into real estate speculators who keep hold of their property rather than putting it on the market in expectation that prices will rise. With little inventory on the market, values indeed shot skyward, which only fed the frenzy of speculation further. And as I write this, values in Seattle are rising the fastest of any major city in the country. At some point the bubble will burst, and the local economy will suffer.

My campaign came from a good place in my heart. I was honoring the Conti in the process, running a campaign as a way to give back to the community what it had given us. But it was not sustainable. It was not only the issue of my residency that began to scuttle my campaign, but the reality was that I had taken a bite from a side of beef that was not settling well with my body. It was the wrong time to run for office, and we had no help at home. My wife and I both had to work to keep our incomes above water, and as lecturers at the university, which means low pay, this was almost impossible to do. In the end, I had to suspend my campaign. A few folks were upset, some surprised, but I was relieved. It had become a burden I could no longer bear.

The legacy of the Conti had to live on in people's hearts. And it had to do so without my help or encouragement, or that of anyone else. It was noble, perhaps, of me to wish so, but it was probably also self-serving. No one individual plans and runs a legacy; it's an organic process by which sincere people realize the value of a place and in their thoughts and memories do their best to keep it alive and pass this sentiment down to others.

During my brief campaign I rediscovered Jane Jacobs. I had read about her before briefly, but in the urgency of the campaign I reflected upon her own legacy and her imprint on Greenwich Village in New York. Robert Moses, for decades the great builder of New York, had amassed great power that he converted into projects. Indefatigable, charming, cunning, and a brilliant user of power, Moses exemplified the spirit that built America. He had a vision of Manhattan as not only a world-class metropolis, but one that was amenable to the automobile. He saw cities as locations that could be traversed by cars. He saw little value in neighborhoods in the city, some of which he considered slums. So, he condemned them, rammed highways through them and called it progress. When he tried to do the same for Greenwich, Jane Jacobs stood up. She organized protests against it, and by some miracle, in a vote in city hall, stopped Moses. A brilliant account of the battle is highlighted in Anthony Flint's *Wrestling with Moses*.[1] Her vision of a city and its neighborhood is one of human relationship in a kind of musical flow of interactions and daily activities. A city is not for cars any more than it's for developers or city officials or the government; it's for its residents. It's for people that see in built environments a call to their humanity and to their social relationships. This was certainly the case of my Greek

Multi-tasking is a familiar requirement for a small business owner. Here Demetre Lagos serves as a cashier, among his many other duties.

village; what sustained the community was its human-to-human contact. The great destruction of the village that I discovered during my dissertation research was television, since it took villagers away from the café society and kept them at home watching the boob tube.

Cooking Greek, Becoming American

There is no mechanism to keep social institutions like the Conti alive, no law, no city ordinance, no government decree, no referendum. It is a place that lived because my family (my mother, father, and brother, and, less so, me) put in the many hours, the sweat and grit, the pain, the angst, and lack of sleep and sheer determination to make it happen. And we certainly did not do so out of some grand strategic conviction or because we were a noble family destined to supply the community with much valued social capital. It was never that, nor could it ever be; it was much simpler—it was our job, it was our daily bread. From that came its institutionalization as a community center. Because the process was an accidental one, my family was as surprised as anyone at the outpouring of sadness and grief that it was going away. Many reacted as if a death had happened in their family, and indeed it had. A tradition was about to go away—for those who ate there before or after going to church, or worked there, then started families and saw their own children become servers at the Conti, or simply came to the restaurant to eat lunch on a regular basis, the Conti served as a reminder that consistency, not change, could be good. That even as life never stands idle, there are some markers in it that remain the same in the face of change, and in doing so, contribute mightily to it.

But creating this is not a recognizable career path. Students in high school do not suddenly announce they want to become practitioners and promoters of social capital and the owners of important third places like the Conti. Our culture attunes itself to wealth and status. There is an interesting study related in Robert D. Putnam's *Bowling Alone*, a seminal work on social capital, he relates an interesting study done between two demographically identical communities (income, education, racial composition, etc.) except for one factor—one community exhibited traits of high social capital (neighbors lent each other their lawn mowers, there were block parties, etc.), while the other had low social capital. Guess which one had fewer health problems?

What I failed to see at the time of the restaurant's sale was that despite the many tensions of keeping the operation alive, we were generally happier as a family. Since the Conti ended, we as family members have gone our separate ways with little expectation that we will ever come together again. The Conti was glue for the local neighborhood, but also for our own family. We had no idea that its closing would impact us as much as it did.

So why not start another Continental? If only. A charming idea, this, but with each passing day, it becomes more and more difficult. And with each passing day, other restaurants come to fill in for the Conti to our former customers. We might, if we are lucky, gain some of them back were we to resurrect the operation, but there is no guarantee they would come back. We would have to compete for customers as any new restaurant does, and I am not sure I am willing to take that gamble.

For a while after he sold the place, my dad considered starting a company manufacturing some items that he had perfected at the Conti—namely the lentil soup, tzatziki, hummus, and even his excellent "loukaniko" Greek sausage. And there was talk that even I could spearhead this, as I had tried to do for a short time in the early 1990s with distributing the loukaniko. By this point, I had gone to other projects—mostly focusing on my academic career and the writings that were now emanating from me. Raising a child is difficult enough; growing and raising a restaurant on top of this is too much for me. I no longer have that kind of stamina. I recognize my limits now.

So, the Conti is now part of history, where it shall remain forever. Perhaps someone out there might try to resurrect it, and if so, I would be happy to see it alive again, and flourishing. I would like to order "Taso's Breakfast" again; somehow, making it at home is not the same. If this were to happen, I would like to make some suggestions for the new and perhaps improved Conti.

One. Greek cuisine is one of the healthiest in the world. So, the new Conti must begin with a commitment to serving healthy, nutritious food with real ingredients, not the imitation variety that is good for food suppliers (and high profits), but not for our bodies. Offer organic as much as possible. Brown rice instead of white. There should not be any Crisco in the kitchen anywhere. Only butter and olive oil should be used for cooking. And not vegetable oil for the deep fryer, which I would do away with, but if the new owner insisted on using some kind of oil to keep the Greek fries alive, then use peanut oil, or soybean oil, or corn oil, or something considerably healthier than vegetable oil. Eggs for omelets should be organic, and never (and I am happy that the Conti never did this) add milk to the omelet mix as some Greek restaurants do today— milk cheapens the omelet mix and is intended to increase profits. All vegetable ingredients in an omelet should be fresh and organic. Use real butter on the toast instead of the human-made kind we used (I never could convince my old man to change this, an argument I never won).

Two. Labor costs in an eatery are the highest single expenditure, despite the fact that restaurants pay only minimum wage. We had between twenty and twenty-five employees at any given moment. Giving everyone a decent wage is hard. My father supplanted decent treatment for high wages; there were a few employees who had been with us decades, and they received a living wage. Others received the bare minimum, yet they continued to work there while working other jobs because they loved our family and the environment of the Conti. But the new owner must decide if she wants to provide decent wages to employees or focus on the bottom line. I suggest she focus on living wages, even if that means fewer employees. Some restaurants solve the problem of wages by staying open only part of the day, say for breakfast and lunch, but not dinner, or dinner but not breakfast and lunch. Decent wages may mean cutting expenses in other areas—rent, or electricity (going solar?), or fancy décor. We had simple, aging décor, and it didn't really bother most people. It bothered me, but I regard that now as youthful stupidity on my part.

Three. It is absolutely imperative that restrooms always be kept clean and tidy. My mother cleaned the restrooms each and every morning because that's where the soul of an eatery is. Customers don't have to go back to the kitchen to know how clean and efficient it is; they only have to go to the bathroom to see what the owner's definition of cleanliness is. And I recommend strong-powered toilets that flush with vigor, not the home variety that plug up too often. Urinals should never smell and always have ice in them. Bathrooms should be decorated, and if customers once in a while make off with a picture or other items from a bathroom, well, let them; it's part of the expense of running a restaurant. Customers steal silverware, too, and it's not a really big deal.

Four. The menu. What does the new Conti offer its customers? Well, the traditional standbys: omelets, lunch platters, dinner entrees, such as dolmathes, souvlaki, mousaka, and other traditional fare, but also experimental new dishes involving lamb, fish, and herbs. All employees in the restaurant should be encouraged to come up with innovative dishes, not just the cooks. Innovation should be at the heart of the new Conti; it should offer customers dishes that they simply do not and cannot get anywhere else. The greatness of my family agreeing to Taso's Breakfast was not because it's such a brilliant dish, but because we recognized that it would be a popular one when people began to see me eating it and ordered it themselves. I felt special to have one of my own creations on the menu, and it happened completely accidentally. This is good management, and it cannot be substituted. Another family, another management might have simply ignored this, but we didn't, and it's a credit to us for being so perceptive.

Five. Customers need good food, but they also crave attention and human warmth. In these pages I have repeatedly emphasized the human element to running a restaurant. I recently finished reading *Call Me Roger*, brilliantly written by Albert Lee.[2] In it he discussed the ill-fated leadership of General Motors by a humanoid named Roger B. Smith. He was a financial genius who had no interest in developing his humanity; he routinely gave himself and his top executives yearly bonuses but regarded many of his 750,000 workers (particularly factory ones) as overpaid. He seemed perfectly capable of going out of his way to insult or anger tens of thousands of his employees. He had a habit of completely ignoring someone sitting right in front of his desk in his office, or not speaking to another person, or never once looking up from his desk. Simple acts of humanity—genuinely smiling when the customer enters the door, being pleasant at all times during the meal, thanking customers when they leave—are not very costly and do not require the same level of physical and mental endurance as digging a sidewalk in 105°F weather as I witnessed in the summer of 2004 prior to the start of the Athens Olympic and Paralympic Games. Every customer who walked into the Conti could be guaranteed a smile and a warm greeting. In time, even a cantankerous soul like me came to appreciate the sheer value of this. Think about how rushed and frazzled we all are in our lives, and consider the value of walking into a restaurant and being greeted with humanity and sincerity. Life suddenly becomes much better at that moment. Why belabor this point? It's strangely uncommon.

Six. Owning a business requires dealing with dozens of salespeople who enter the establishment and will attempt to sell you on a product or service. After all, during business hours, the door is open, and anyone can walk in—friend, foe, or salesperson. Most food ordering was done through a small coterie of sales folks who came to the restaurant regularly. Most were decent people; some tried to outfox my father, who always did the restaurant's ordering. While there are now online systems that take care of this, my father preferred to deal with human beings and I recommend the same. Any food item that enters the restaurant must be accounted for, yet also have its quality vouched for. All ingredients should be wholesome and fresh. As enticing as it is to substitute the expedient and cheap, it is a mistake to believe that this is anything other than greed. A restaurant is a mini factory without the robots, although this is changing. Every dish served is made to order; restaurants are not usually assembly lines. But this manufacturing process must be based on quality, not quantity. It must focus on top ingredients because every human being deserves to eat the best food.

Seven. There are challenges to running a restaurant. There are rude customers. Accidents (i.e., broken teeth from biting on a souvlaki, spilled soups and coffee, etc.) occur. When hundreds come in the door every day, the law of the universe dictates that not all will go perfectly well. Keeping calm and pleasant is a must in these situations, even as it is difficult (I found it hard, but it got a bit easier over time). Ultimately, there must be forgiveness. Human beings change. The jerk today becomes the decent one tomorrow. I should know: I fit that category. Being angry at a customer leaves a stain of evil that is not easily wiped away. If you ask someone to leave, you can at least try to be humane about it. All interactions should have this mark of decency about them, however troubling and incendiary they could be. The Conti was good at this practice, and this vital tradition should continue.

Eight. It's a family. Customers. Employees. Salespeople. Vendors. Even the health inspector. Everyone is in it together. People come to rely on the restaurant for their livelihood, and this should never be dismissed flippantly. No one likes having a health inspector, but such folks provide a valuable service to the restaurant. In the universe that is the restaurant, the new Conti accepts its role as a community institution from the start and operates on the premise that it serves its customers and stakeholders, and not the other way around. The man who comes to fix the refrigerator is as much a part of the restaurant as the regular customer who comes five times a week. If the new owner needs to be reminded of this, she should make a sign with big block letters and place it in her office.

The most important legacy of the Conti is the one we had no clue about until well after we sold the place. The biggest challenge for an immigrant is to assimilate into the new adopted culture. Village life is nothing like what we faced in America; it is not as if we arrived from a developed country, we hailed from a nation struggling to overcome its past deficiencies and one that after World War II plunged into civil war. Its economy and social and political institutions had collapsed. It was not a nation fully prepared for the modern era. Primarily rural and agricultural, Greece struggled to industrialize, with uneven success. Its biggest product was the hundreds of thousands of emigrants who left its mountainous landscape in search of better lives in Europe, North America, Africa, and Australia. This has been more or less true since the 1880s, when spreading factories created demand for low-skilled labor that Greeks (like many other Southeastern Europeans) were happy to fill.

Immigration continues to be a feature of the American experience. Yet, assimilation of these foreigners into the American fabric has always been the challenge: How to convert hundreds of different ethnic groups into Americans? Various national policies have been tried—from night school to various methods of hygiene that suggest faint elements of racism and acculturation (our American culture is superior to all foreign ones). These policies of assimilation (repeated in English-speaking countries such as Australia, South Africa, Canada, etc.) for the most part did not really succeed because forced acculturation is really an amputation of one's identity. This may be good politics for some in the United States, since it assumes that less social tension will result from assimilation, but for most immigrants, replacing one identity with another simply does not work.

We clung to our Greek identity as a matter of survival in our new homeland. Replacing this identity with a new American one was asking us to commit suicide. Keeping some semblance of our old ways was the best method by which we could hold some balance in our lives, without being psychically overwhelmed. The assimilation policies were created by those who were not immigrants and were in response to demands that aliens become Americans no matter the social and psychological costs to the immigrants themselves. Rather than leaving the process to take place organically, giving the immigrant the freedom to choose for himself, past and current assimilist policies have shoved America down immigrants' throats. Many Americans intuitively know this from their travels abroad. It is not uncommon to hear travelers proclaim that they feel more "American" when they are in a foreign country, suddenly coming face to face with a different culture that visibly exposes their own and makes them conscious of their ways. So with immigrants to the United States.

Our best tool of assimilation was the Continental. We had no idea at the time, but upon reflection it has revealed itself to be the case. Work (and, in the case of my brother and me, schooling) had more impact in bringing us closer to the American way than any forced policy of acculturation ever could. It did this primarily because of the sanctity of work itself. When a restaurant, or any immigrant operation, is busy, no one cares whether one has an accent or not. When we face a hundred or so hungry customers abruptly filling the restaurant, whatever elements of identity reside in me at that moment pale or become trivial under the demands of feeding them. Simply, can we do the job or not?

Over time we took on new identities tied to the Conti, and, by extension, to the United States, as a natural outgrowth of the demands of the restaurant. It was not a process that we designed or were even aware of (as with the Conti as a community institution, knowledge about this assimilation process came from my immigrant studies), but it is one that left its mark on us. I cannot precisely tell you the moment we felt "American," that is a personal process (mine came in the days after 9/11), but I can state unequivocally that it indeed happened.

Not all operations are alike, thus a non-service business might have created conditions where assimilation was slower or less intense. Certainly, interacting with our customers as we did on a daily basis at the Conti sped up our acceptance into American society. Had we been working in a coal mine or an automobile factory it might have taken longer. Work also brought us dignity and the satisfaction that we were in charge of our own destiny. We learned English because we had to. Forcing people to learn English is simply not the same.

Not all immigrants can buy into a restaurant, or another service operation, so it may be unrealistic to propose that assimilation be left to take place organically and naturally. But the knowledge that this is possible in such environments provides some awareness that it can happen and with stunning results. Had the Conti not existed for our family, I do not believe we would have adapted as we did; my mother would not have become the efficient and outstanding server/manager of the place, and my father likely would have remained a struggling plumber going from one plugged toilet to the next with little regard for embracing the ways of the new land.

Chapter Eight

America's Promise to All

It is easier to be an American than to become one. When my family moved to the United States, we struggled to make sense of our new home and to find our footing. We came with little preparation for the difficulties the move entailed. We left a small community of about a thousand folks who more or less knew each other and came to a land where the opposite was true. We had no idea how we would survive in this new culture. Everything was new and terrifying for us. There was an innocence and naiveté about us. I noticed the "Dead End" signs on some streets and thought America was an extraordinarily philosophical place—reminding everyone about their final destiny in street signs. Learning to speak was particularly difficult.

For several years we lived in limbo, trying not to be overwhelmed by circumstances, but being so nonetheless. We had no guides to help us. Even those Greek Americans who arrived in Seattle before us, a few from our village, even, did help, but they could not be with us every day—they had their own struggles to overcome. So, we were on our own. Every day became a week, and every week a month. Time dragged on; at times, it even stood still. All the markers that existed for me in my previous village life—my home, my school, my friends, my routines—were now history, and I had to find new ones. No one told me how.

We could pretend we came to a better life, certainly a more comfortable one—we lived with my uncle who was becoming a more popular dentist. From an apartment to a small house to a lakeside home with swimming pool in only a matter of a few years. A swimming pool! Yet, beneath the success were uncertainty and doubt. Most immigrants do not spend any time mentally preparing for the move to the United States. All I recall was that Uncle John visited the village one day, and then some months later my father told my brother and me that we would be going to America. Other villagers exalted our impending journey. "Gold in the streets!" they told us we would find about "Ameriki." It seemed incongruous to us. But there was no one to tell us about the difficulty of learning a new language and adjusting to the real culture there.

I kept hearing about the greatness of America that last year in the village and in time it became a magical place for me. Eden on Earth. But I liked the village and wondered why we had to leave. What would happen to my best friend George? And the little girl I was in love with next door, Ioanna? And flying my kite in spring? And going to the most beautiful beach in the world, Tsilaro, in summer where we swam in the day, slept in the afternoon, and listened to stories under the stars, with lapping waves at night? And my grandmother, who would not come with us, how could we leave her to live alone?

There were many questions, but they were not being answered. My parents either had no answer or worried about other matters. The political situation in Greece in the mid–1960s worsened. Politics have always been unstable in Greece, ever since it became an independent nation from the Ottoman Empire in 1830. But things took a turn for the worse as conservative and liberal forces that had divided politics for decades turned up the heat on each other. On April 21, 1967, we woke up to the democratically elected government being ousted by a band of colonels in a military takeover of the country.

For the first time in my young life, I saw fear in my father's eyes. He had never been afraid of anything and had a reputation for courage and strength (as a hard worker, no one could beat "Londos!"), but suddenly he stopped going to the cafés in the evening and huddled at home with us. It was strange to have him spend his nights at home, and huddle with my mother and grandmother.

The atmosphere in the village changed. A sudden chill tinged the air, and social activity abruptly dropped. There were fewer celebrations in the cafés and church attendance rose as villagers became more "traditional" and "conservative" in their outlook. Since the colonels decreed that any group of more than three getting together constituted a demonstration, and therefore could be arrested, one avoided small crowds. Liberals had to now watch their backs.

My father's side of the family had a reputation for being liberals. His brother was a well-known socialist who had been imprisoned and tortured for his political beliefs. My paternal grandfather had been a socialist leader in the community that, and when the Nazis swept into Greece in 1941, was summarily killed along with his wife, my grandmother. On the other side of the political divide, Greek guerrillas accused my maternal grandfather of being a collaborator with the invaders. While it was not true, he nevertheless paid for the lie with his life, and my grandmother was forced to raise three children and a newborn. I grew up without a grandfather and only one grandmother. Other children don't even have a granny, so I suppose I was lucky.

My father had his own brand of politics, and was a liberal, no doubt, but he was not a political animal like Uncle Nick. Yet, he knew that life would change for the worse and whatever plans had been made for us to emigrate to the United States abruptly took on more urgency. Phone calls were made to the U.S. and decisions made, to which my brother and I were not privy. Life had become unpleasant, and even we children felt it, or saw it. One day, out of the blue, a small convoy of Army jeeps roared into the village, completely unsettling everyone, and stopped outside one house near the central square. Soldiers jumped out and stormed into one house, arresting the father of the family. As he was led away, other troops went into the house, grabbed furniture and dropped it from the second-floor landing. A few of us kids saw this, but there were no adults around to witness it; all were locked inside their homes. My father feared that he would be next.

My mother restricted how much time we spent playing, so it became a strange summer. That summer in 1967 I found myself at my grandmother's brother's goat-herding operation in the mountains where I slept in a bed with four others, and I had to get up early to help tend the goats. It was not my idea of fun and took me away from my beloved books, but my parents decided I was safer with "Barba Vangello" in the wilds of the mountains than in the village. It was the same place, incidentally, where the guerrilla fighters hid during World War II.

By late August plans had been set into motion—we would be leaving Greece. I attended only a few days of school before one day we got our suitcases ready and headed for Athens. My grandmother came with us. We would spend a few days there with my dad's sister and then fly to the United States. Athens was a swelling metropolis then, a growing tourist hub despite the military coup in place, yet, it was not my village, and I was not happy there. I already felt homesick, but there was no turning back. My father tried to make the time in Athens as happy as possible, although he still feared arrest. We went to the Acropolis (my grandmother refused to go, saying, "Why should I see a bunch of ruins?!"). Time sped up, and by Friday, we were ready to leave. Taxis were ordered, and we went to the airport, at the time located inside the city near the bay. It was painful to say goodbye to the many relatives who gathered there that morning. It took an eternity. I was emotionally numb; forget that I had never flown before, what terrified me was that we were entering a new unknown world. I had been asked to leave the comforting familiarity of my home for the unknown.

We checked our luggage, there was more crying, and the relatives watched us go through security. Soldiers with machine guns patrolled the airport. We were placed in a waiting area, and then a bus came to pick everyone up and drive us to the parked plane on the tarmac. As we got off the bus and were about to board the plane, a thin man in a billowing white shirt came running up to my father. He pulled him aside so none of us could hear what he was saying. But I saw the sparkle in my father's eyes disappear and be replaced by worry.

The official put us back on the bus, and we had to go back inside the terminal. It seemed, so my father explained to us, that there was a problem with our paperwork. Our relatives were watching this from the roof of the airport, and after more discussion between my father and Mr. White Shirt, we were instructed to come back the next day. We were stunned. You mean, do this again the next day?

No one slept. My father was up all night, talking to my mother. It was much later that I learned there was nothing wrong with our paperwork; the man stopped us because he wanted a bribe. So, my father had to scramble to get cash, and when we arrived at the airport the next day, Saturday, he met Mr. White Shirt and suddenly, the paperwork was fine. We said our goodbyes again to our relatives—strangely muted this time—went back to the same waiting area, the same bus, and the same plane on the tarmac. This time, we managed to make it up the steps of the plane without anyone stopping us. I took one last look at Greece and ducked inside.

Flying was a new experience for me. We would rise above the earth, head for Brussels, and from there to New York, before our last skip to Seattle. Being served by attractive, articulate flight attendants was an entirely new experience. There was food and drink. Brussels was a brief stop (I don't recall whether we even got out of the airplane), but within a short time we were back in the air, now flying above the Atlantic. The sun stayed with us all day. We slept and ate and spent time with our thoughts. We even tried to learn a little bit of English (I don't recall if it was from a book or just my father teaching us, but I picked up the word "No").

In New York, we got off the airplane and waited about six hours in a large waiting area. In front of me at one point, an African American janitor was mopping the floor, the first time I had seen a black person. I was fascinated, although I wondered if it bothered him that I stared at him for the entire time he was near us, which must have been well over an hour. I simply could not take my eyes off him. Finally, we got on a plane and began the last leg of the journey. For the first time, I sat next to the window.

First impressions last because they indent our memories with intensity. The first image of Seattle that startled me was the vast expanse of lights. Miles and miles of lights, a vast carpet of lights that stretched into eternity. In the village, I could see lights in the distance of another village, but mostly there was darkness, so it was odd to face a landscape of lights that never ended. The plane descended smoothly, and we were on the ground. It was evening, sometime around eight. Uncle John waited for us. Soon we were in his car and driving north, confirming what I had seen from the air was indeed real—the city stretched forever. Those lights were not in my imagination.

We came to the Viking Apartments off Aurora in Lynnwood. As we got out of the car, taking our little luggage with us and climbing up the steps to the second-floor landing, we came to the front door of Uncle John's apartment. My father suddenly got down on his knees and kissed the ground in front of the door, startling all of us. Uncle Sam, a first cousin on my paternal grandfather's side of the family, waited inside for us. Tears of joy to be in America were soon replaced by more mundane things, like me having to go to the bathroom and being exhausted. I wanted to sleep, but my parents made us stay up late. Finally, it seemed near midnight, we had a chance to catch some sleep. Uncle John had readied for us by getting two bunk beds, with me taking the top one, and we would go to sleep as Greeks, but wake up Sunday morning as Americans, or, at least, Americans-in-training.

For breakfast, we were used to my mother or grandmother milking the goats, bringing the small pot of fresh milk into the kitchen and boiling it, whereupon we swallowed it down with a piece of bread with honey on it. But now, welcome to America, it would be different—cereal and cold cow's milk. Neither tasted particularly good to me. That morning, as much as I tried to like it, and being as hungry as I was, I could not eat. Uncle John left for church that morning and so Demetre and I managed to eat some bread for breakfast, so we managed not to starve.

The next day we were in school.

I was in elementary school, and my brother in middle school. In other words, worlds apart. My brother was more social and outgoing, so he quickly made friends. I was the opposite. That fateful first day Uncle

John dropped me off, and I was taken by a teacher to a classroom of cheerful white kids all staring at me. The school must have been prepared for my arrival for within a few minutes after arriving in the class, I was led out to another room where I was to face a special education teacher for my learning. What bothered me about this arrangement was that I never had a chance to get to meet my new classmates. This was repeated for a few months; arrive at school, go to my home room, and a few minutes after the bell rang, I was led out to the empty room with the single teacher. Only at recess did we meet, and as the "special ed" student, I was shunned.

This mercifully came to an end when a few weeks into my ordeal, Uncle John announced we were moving to a house. Having five people in a small apartment was not working. This meant a new school. I had always arrived at my former school in shorts, but when I did that at the new school, I was sent home. Uncle John had walked me to school and when we arrived at my fourth-grade home room, Mrs. Inscho, the teacher, took one look at my bare legs and insisted that I wear long pants in her classroom. So back home I went, changed my pants and returned to the school alone. Uncle John left to go to his dental practice.

I knocked gingerly on the door and Mrs. Inscho came to lead me inside. She took me to the front of the room and introduced me to the students. At that moment, the recess bell rang, and the room suddenly emptied. I looked at the teacher, who signaled for me to join the other kids outside. So, I went out and joined them. When I arrived at the playground, I was surrounded by other kids. They shouted at me, but I had no idea what they were saying. So, I kept shouting back, "No, no, no." Each time I did so, it seemed to rouse their laughter, which grew and grew in intensity. When it was about to reach a fever pitch, the bell rang, and we all stopped to head back to class. Years later when I was able to speak English, I asked one of the kids (David Robinson) who was there that morning. "David, what were you asking me then?" He looked at me and smiled. "Oh, the usual," he replied coyly. "Do you eat in Greece? Do you like girls? Are you smart?"

It took me two years to feel confident speaking English. Mrs. Inscho could have and should have flunked me for failing all the exams and not turning in my homework. Graciously and generously, she gave me Ds and let me graduate to fifth grade. In fifth, I got a few Cs, and by the sixth, I was doing well enough to earn some Bs. She was under no obligation to do so, and it is unlikely it would have been allowed in Greece, especially given my family's political past. But in America, there were no questions asked about my family's political history. It didn't matter. I was now in a new land and was becoming, however slowly, part of its fabric.

By the time we entered the restaurant business, I felt more connected and a part of my new homeland, and I began to cherish its ways, even as I missed the village. When I returned briefly in 1976 for a summer visit, the village was no longer the same, and whatever image I had of it had vanished. My friends had grown up and pursued their own lives. Many remembered me, but they had more important matters on their minds. The junta had been overthrown, and democracy returned. Everyone seemed weary and spent and had little time to celebrate my return. I felt let down, as if my special home had rejected me. I returned to America to that summer to start college, but in doing so I realized that I could never go back to Greece. That door was now closed, and I had better learn to adapt to Seattle.

I always escaped into movies. If there was one way to tamp down the pain of my immigrant-ness, it was through cinema. I had fallen in love with it at four after seeing my first movie, and by the time I was in my late teens, it provided me with a refuge from my cultural confusion as a Greek American and to what my identity really was. In movies, there was no such dilemma; I was free to explore my private flights of fancy by delving into the world of drama. I fell in love with screenwriting. I read and re-read *Chinatown* by Robert Towne, even copied its every single word by hand to learn the craft. When I met Towne in Seattle as a part-time film critic for the campus student newspaper, *The Daily*, the goosebumps on my arms were clearly visible.

Here was fantastic literature, yet not widely available, or even treasured in college English courses (changing now). More than that, it was a special craft that I knew I had to master because it allowed me to fashion my own stories. In these tales I could spin worlds that were so different from my own; there were no immigrants and natives, only plots and protagonists, antagonists and other characters. It was a world that I could control, based on my imagination. It was not dictated to me by others; I was in charge. I commanded my life, not like the real world, where I felt beholden to my family and eventually to the restaurant.

This indulgence could never have been allowed in Greece; as a product of the countryside, without any connections or benefactors to help me, I was shut out from such a world. In America, there were possibilities. In America, even an immigrant could write scripts and succeed. My hero was Steve Tesich (né Stojan Tešić), who was born in what is now Serbia and immigrated with his family when he was fourteen. He became a playwright, and one of his scripts became a popular movie, *Breaking Away*, which also won an Academy Award for best original screenplay.

There was always a promise about this country that allowed even the less fortunate a chance. And this was the greatness of this country: that there was always a chance that something, anything might happen. It might, and usually does, involve luck, but as long as there was the chance, there was hope. I realized that the greatness of America came from it being a sieve; it let in strangers and the unwanted from other countries and fashioned them, somehow, into productive citizens. In those times it chose to close the drawbridges and not let anyone in, it was the poorer for it. When it resumed letting folks in, its wealth—economic, social, cultural, spiritual—increased.

It was impossible for us to buy into a restaurant in Greece as easily as my father did in America. The entrepreneurial obstacles are too great in the old country, which is why so many Greeks leave and why they do so well elsewhere. More Greeks live outside the country than inside it, a fact not lost on those who remain. It seems that there's a regular drain; rather than focusing its energy on building up Greece, the country yearly loses some of its best talent to other nations. And these nations become wealthier for it.

What would have become of my family had we remained in Greece? My father would certainly have remained a coal miner and farmer as long as his body held up; my mother would have continued as housewife; my brother would not have created a rich extended family; and my sister would likely not have become a tenured professor in California married to a successful real estate developer. These accomplishments took place in America. Few other places in world, if any, perhaps would have allowed or even encouraged such success. And would a Continental have existed anywhere else? It grew out of the social unrest of the 1960s and the rich history of the U–District, or out of a specific time and place, and to replicate it somewhere else would have made it not the same. Would another family have contributed to its success as we did? Since my father sold it to a family that had no interest in keeping it the same format tells me such a fate seems impossible.

Now that I have lived in America most of my life, several decades, what does it mean to me? If I could tell my close-to-nine-year-old self back in the village wondering but anxious about the family move to America, what would I tell him? What advice would I offer?

I would brace him for stark change and difficulty but assure him that he would be going to a magical place. It would be filled with many other children like him, who left their homes and their friends and their school and their habits—only to enter a strange world that at first does not make sense but in a few years becomes a place of vast opportunity. Steve Jobs was born to a Lebanese immigrant father who gave him up for adoption, and he grew up to be a great impacter of society. Albert Einstein left Nazi Germany and spent his remaining and productive years in the United States. Countless others left their own misery to find a new and better place on these shores. And you too will find comfort and joy here, I would say to him. But it will not come easy, and you may even hate the place for some years when you first arrive.

But America makes its influence drip by drip, without knowing it, every day bringing an immigrant closer and closer to realizing her potential. There is competition, to be sure, there are trials and tribulations, no doubt, but there are also moments where dreams are fashioned and pursued and, if one is lucky, achieved. To do so takes grit and desire, talent and fortune, maturity and wisdom. America will take a chance on you, I would tell the boy, just as you took a chance on her. It's reciprocal. There are few one-way streets in America. Have faith in yourself, I would add, and do not let worry and anxiety overwhelm you. Life will be new and strange and even distorting, but that is only the outside shell; inside is a rich, delicious fruit waiting to be savored.

The boy is unlikely to listen to me since children rarely can and do, but at least I may provide him the knowledge that all will be well. All is not lost. Life will continue, and even be better. Then I would take him by the hand and walk him up to a small lookout point above the village near the school where he spent many happy but also miserable moments. I would remind him of what happened in this spot just a few years before when he had seen his first movie. He told his parents that he wanted to make films, just like what he startlingly had witnessed. They smiled and even patted him on the head, not realizing he was serious.

So, he did what any near-five-year-old would do—he began to tag along after the man, also named Taso, who brought the films to the village each Friday. He knew what time Film Taso arrived and waited for him. In a short while, he became Film Taso's assistant—putting up the advertisement on a wall in the village square (the poster always different, but the glossy black and white photos that accompanied it the same). He became familiar with the drill: Film Taso arriving in late afternoon, the young assistant (me) putting up the advertisement while he set up the chairs, screen, and film projector on the flat roof over the café.

Then sometime around six or seven in the evening, he got into his white Chevrolet car with a speaker on the hood, and slowly drove around the village streets announcing the film for the night. One day he asked me to join him on these rounds. It was my first time in an automobile (I had been on a tractor before, but not in a car). I was thrilled. I felt the raw emotion of realizing I was becoming closer to him and that perhaps he would grant me my wish: that I could make films just like the ones he showed the villagers.

He traversed the village and I watched him as he spoke into the microphone inside the car. He had a rich voice, and it carried to the hillside homes. Then he wound up a narrow, treacherous road bending through the heart of the village and came to the lookout point. He parked the car there, made one last announcement, and then turned off the engine. My moment arrived.

I was nervous and felt my heart beating faster than I had ever known before, even more so than when I was with my beloved Ioanna. I had to be strong, I told myself. The special moment had come. My hands and knees trembled and for it seemed as if my throat was too dry to speak. How could I tell him?

Finally, after what seemed eternity, but no doubt was just a few beats, I turned to Taso and asked the fateful question: "Taso," I began in my high-pitched wail, "I have helped you all these weeks, and I wonder if you would now allow me to make the films."

He had been lost in some thought, staring out at the village, yet he immediately turned to me, smiling gently but telling me in words that I could not forget: "Taso, I don't make the films. I only show them!"

My heart sank. I would remind my boy self of this moment as we stand on this same lookout point. "Guess what," I would say. "That dream could not be achieved here, but you will go to a place where it can."

CHAPTER NINE

A Place at the Table

We traditionally think of a school as a place where formal learning occurs—with books, exams, grades, degrees, etc. We all know learning is not limited to schools but takes place in a wide variety of locations. I have learned as much about teaching from formal classes as I have from watching how my daughter processes information. She has been, in fact, my supreme teacher: teaching me patience, making learning fun, and discovering what keeps her attention.

The restaurant was a school for the family. We learned to be Americans, or, at least, Americans as defined by the local community. Had the operation been located in Wyoming, we may have a different experience of Americahood right now. The great diversity of the country both amazes and unnerves. The eatery also taught us the value of hard work. This is a phrase with many different meanings. The one I refer to involves an appreciation of physical labor's importance to our development into productive human beings. No doubt a majority of the physical work in an eatery is tedious and thankless, usually at the same time. Busing tables, cleaning floors, cleaning dishes, cooking over a grill—none of these are noble in and of themselves, except in the knowledge that a business is maintained, a customer is fed, a place is kept clean, the trust of our clientele to put into their mouths food we produced is sustained. We have lost the ability to appreciate hard work as a daily reality; we prefer the easy way, a lifestyle of comfort and ease. Hard work is simply too damn hard. In the hierarchy of social status, jobs that require physical work are at the bottom, left for the less educated, the immigrants, the poor, and the disadvantaged. It is a curious fact that in blue zones, or those places in the world where people live the longest, one of the attributes to longevity is physical exertion. The story of my busing tales at the busy restaurant next to the Old World in Los Angeles indicates how much this ethic was inculcated into my very being.

Ethnic restaurants are great equalizers. They are visible proof of the commonality of our humanity; they demonstrate the power of unity, when customers and servers and cooks and hosts are all engaged in the common cause of satisfying human hunger. In the moment and in the space, hierarchies, such as they are, are temporarily abolished. Much as we trust and have faith in communion during mass, when we open our bodies to the body and blood of the Christ figure, we engage in a kind of "holy" union in the dining room of a restaurant with its proprietors and the food they provide us.

Restaurants are special. And they are so for the identities they grant. I reflect on my shyness and my struggle to overcome it, which the Conti helped. I have been shy all my life; my mother told me that I was a very docile, shy child. I wasn't too shy to hang out with the pretty little girl living next door, but my life was an internal one. When we arrived in America, my shyness went into overdrive. I hid from the world because it was too strange for my liking and I yearned desperately to go back, as I've noted. I knew I had a severe problem, especially speaking in front of people. Working in the back of the restaurant did not help it; in fact, it made it worse. One day my brother asked me to step in as a manager on a sleepy afternoon and left me to be in charge of the whole dining area.

A customer in a new suit entered and sat. He ordered a bowl of faki and pita bread. It was my first experience being a server. I warmed the pita in the kitchen myself, poured the bowl of soup, and started out to the dining area. The carpet separated the dining room from the servers' area, and even though I had stepped on it thousands of times before, on this day, somehow, I forgot it was there. So, I tripped on it. As the customer sat at a table not far from the servers' area, this meant that, as fate would have it, my fall caused the pita to land on the floor but the bowl of faki to land on his groin. It was hot. He was not pleased, both for heating his private parts and ruining his suit. I apologized profusely, he left to dine somewhere else, and I paid for his dry cleaning bill. It was an inauspicious start, but it taught me a valuable lesson.

Slowly, I gained my footing and felt comfortable interacting with customers. I grew to even like the attention it brought me, although I had trouble dealing with unruly customers, of which the Conti attracted its fair share. Running a restaurant allows no time to be shy or inhibited; you can't be or you won't survive. When a server calls in sick, the owner is faced with the choice of stepping into the role or shutting down the restaurant with the loss of income this implies. It is not an acceptable choice. Like war in which there is no time to be timid, shyness is not sustainable in a restaurant, and it was on this score that I was forced to step out of my rarified comfort zone of big dreams and intellectual introspection and confront real human beings and all that it entailed. That was a gift, too, that the restaurant gave me, even if at the time I was not particularly happy about it. In fact, I did all I could do to run away from it—pursuing other efforts that in the end proved fruitless and a complete waste of time.

We do not consider an institution to be so gifting; our stereotypical model is of the business that must be fed and nurtured at all times, of Charlie Chaplin's character in *Modern Times* who is fed to the machines of industry and ultimately devoured by them. My conceptualization of institutions like restaurants is of their life-giving nourishment for its participants, customers, and staff alike. In this frame, much (effort, time, energy, hard work, thought, determination, etc.) is put in, but much is also gifted back. Could the family have become Americans as we did any other way? Perhaps, but not to the degree that took place during our time at the Continental.

I grew up an individualist, with an independent streak; I had little regard for institutions and their place in the world. I considered all institutions to be corrupt in one fashion or another; morality in my book rested upon the individual and her moral bearings. Remove individuals, and society is meaningless. So, the praise of institutions is not something I expected to write. Recall my initial view of restaurants as places of meaningless encounters, lacking substance and purpose, spaces of exploitation, particularly low wages, in dead-end jobs that sucked the life of all its participants. This was the cynical view that dominated my thinking and only at the end, when the Greek restaurant ceased, could I reassess my thinking. It was not easy; I gave up cherished thoughts and values that had previously sustained me and opened my awareness to a different way of thinking of the Conti.

What became obvious was that, unbeknownst to me, over time the restaurant formed my identity. Not merely that I too, like the rest of my family, was educated in and ushered into the ways of America, the life lived in America, through working at the restaurant, but that the state of my being had been formed and forged there as well. This is an admission and a confession. It is also a revelation. It says something about me as well as the value of third place. In the wildest part of my imagination, I could not foresee that the restaurant became an anvil upon which my personality developed. This is the great surprise of my life (along with having a family), that a solipsistic, tightly wound, and self-contained soul like me could find meaning in joining the community that the

Conti both reflected and sustained. If you look closely at this paragraph, and all the other paragraphs in this book, you may spot a central truth of my life that developed through the restaurant. It was pointed out to me by a friend. Two prophetic comments were uttered to me that opened my eyes as to who I was, both spoken at the Conti. The first was related to me by a customer. While I rang up his bill, I lamented that my brother had all the wealth and I was a broke artist. The customer shot back and said, "Yes, but you have all the stories." The second comment also came at the restaurant: "You have a lot of 'ands' in your sentences." Go back and reread my words in this book and you find this to be true. "And" is a common word; it is a visible manifestation of a more inclusive personality, one that moved away from self-identity to a larger acceptance of and adaptation to the surrounding world. The Conti taught me to be more community-minded, and this truth becomes visible in my daily and written communication.

Once again, this cannot be said of all restaurants, but I suspect it can be related to many of them. The Continental formed my identity and in mostly positive ways that greatly impacted my life. I am the product of this third-place operation and (and!) visible proof of the importance of cherished institutions in our community. My identity needed formation, and it happened in an unlikely place. It was not merely transactional space (customer seeking food, eating, paying, and leaving) but also an identity space that allowed for deeper communication and interactions to take place. There was deeper meaning in the dining room setting than just the act of eating and drinking. When Fred, a regular customer, came to the Conti in a wheelchair with a group of his friends, his body ravaged by AIDS, for his last meal there; the sight left all of us present in a deeper state of mind. Even now I picture the scene and get quite emotional about it; this man who had become a friend to us was on a high that day. He smiled the whole time, as if in his last few days on Earth he got to come in on a Sunday as he always had, surrounded by his friends, treated with dignity and respect and kindness, and knowing he was cared for. He gave all of us present that day the gift of humanity as well as the gift of dignity and self-respect. He was dying, but his spirit was not. It now lives on in his memory and in these words.

I may be accused of elevating the Conti into a state of near worship, failing to remember that it was also the space of difficult encounters, of Eddie attempting to slash his wrist, of fights and punches to my mother, of disagreements inside and outside the family, of the constant

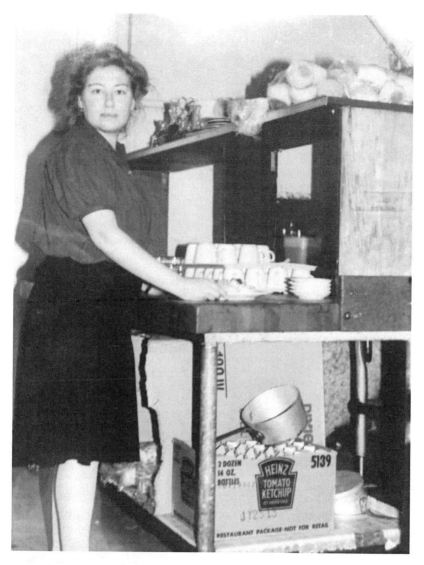

An unidentified server is poised to help a customer. The family always looked for servers who were kind, sincere and hard working. You had to be to survive in a family-operated eatery.

commitment that the restaurant demanded even when we were not capable of giving it. And the robberies too, or the swindlers with bright, shining teeth (one cannot overstate the importance of a good set of teeth in American culture!) who became friends, borrowed money from us, and disappeared. I paint a sacred space without reflecting on the suffering that came with it.

Not at all.

If you've lived on this planet long enough, you do not need to be reminded of life's shortcomings. America is the product of enlightenment, yet its history is riddled with unbridled racism and corrosive caste-ism. It is the oldest modern democracy in the world, yet it is poisoned with inner division and exploitation. Is this what is meant by the quest for a "more perfect union"? I do not need to answer this for you, but I can also tell you that it is a quest, it is a journey to a better world. When we entered the Conti as owners on January 1, 1974, we entered into a kind of covenant that we did not know existed. We embarked on a journey that ultimately altered our family in significant ways: All the personal and professional arcs of the family members reflect the gifts and attributes the Conti gave us. My academic career began at the Continental, with the customer who taught at the University of Washington and promoted my graduate school application. My graduate entry exam scores were not the greatest, but he (and my brother) saw in me potential that I did not. Both encouraged me to stop wandering in the bleak film industry desert and pursue a life that offered more stability and promise for me. The Conti conveniently fed me throughout my grad school years, three times a day. In return I had to give the place my labor and my mind (as coming up with a twenty-five-year celebration of family ownership by rolling back menu prices to 1974, not an original idea but one that proved highly successful, thanks to the mobile phone that turned the place into a madhouse; we eventually ran out of food and could not serve any more customers).

I could focus on the dark side of this journey, and surely there is much, but I must also be aware of the bright part as well. It is the bright side that I mostly portray here because that is the one that I now remember (and care for) most. I do not need to remind anyone that life is pain (as in "life is pain, Highness, and if anyone tells you otherwise, they are selling something!" from *The Princess Bride* movie). You already know this. What you may not know is the other side of this pain, the gift-giving nature of restaurants, that inspired me to write this book.

Throughout this volume, I've talked about the gains my family made. What about the customer, what gifts did she receive? It was a truism of the Conti that roughly 70 percent of our daily business came from folks who regularly ate there. How this figure was obtained is a mystery to me, yet it probably is accurate. On any given day most of the clientele who ate at the Conti were ones known to us; we recognized their faces, many of them we knew by name. My mother even knew what they would order before they opened their mouths; often it was merely seeing a particular customer arriving and sitting that signaled to my mother the order she needed to send to the kitchen. At times it reached comical proportions, in a sort of Kabuki-like theater in which the normal dialogue between a customer and server is simply eliminated and reduced to a few words of exchange.

This familiarity caused problems, too, as when one of our most loyal customers refused to abide by the new non-smoking policy my sister put into effect in 2000. He called my mother a "Nazi!" for which, to his credit, he later apologized. He later got throat cancer and died. And yet we think of him fondly, this smart and erudite man that changed the face of Seattle politics. Most of the time this familiarity bred comfort and stability. In an increasingly anonymous world, it bred the notion that not everything was up for dismemberment and dissolution (which is what made the Conti's closing that much more painful), that some things could remain the same. The Conti as an operation had its fair share of changes, but they were few and far between. Attempts at real changes (offering real feta cheese made from goat's milk, for example) caused a firestorm. Customers found it smelly and expensive.

What kept the place the same, what kept it going as a third place was the family. We remained the same, even as we aged. We became a comfort zone for our regulars—seeing them through growing up, marriages, divorces, career moves up and down, job losses, medical ailments, sudden deaths in the family, and all the other human tragedies. And vice versa; when I went through a breakup and became depressed, one customer came to see me every day for several weeks to talk me through the pain and suffering. She became an angel in my eyes, although I did not fully show her my appreciation for her help.

The Conti was reliable, comfortable; this was due to the family's constant presence. We gave our soul to the place, and the regulars knew it. Those who gathered around the family table (it seems many ethnic restaurants have a family table) knew it too. Every day the conversation that had started many years before continued. There were arguments then, too, to be sure; the politics were too diverse to avoid such occurrences, but there were many more benign discussions than bitter ones. In these family table talks was the Conti was crystallized as an institution and as a force for community. Strangers brought together that over time became friends to us and to each other, even if that friendship was often severely tested by political disagreements.

The family table cannot be replaced online; it was a space people could enter and leave at any moment, and that constancy provided a salve in a culture always up for recreation and change. Regulars came and went; they vented at special times, such as the contested election results in 2000 or when Obama was elected (my brother set up a TV on the pastry side of the restaurant for customers to follow the latest election results as history was made with the first African American president elected). My father always brought out some snack for everyone to eat (free of charge!), and there we all were—gathered together like in cafés of old where such gatherings mattered before television destroyed them. The Conti became an oasis from the growing anonymity of life, where strangers became friends and confidants, and where relations that sustained human lives were expressed and maintained.

Watching and participating in these conversations brought me out of my shell and introduced me to the larger world of humanity (at least, in this tiny corner of the country). Yes, it's possible to have friends, I learned, and it's possible to trust others over time. I joined the conversation and learned to tell stories which only lifted my confidence that helped me get over my fear of public speaking. The teaching the resulted from this would not have been possible. Aside from the career trajectory participating in these conversations provided me, the larger issue remains of what it says about the way human beings interact in today's world. The value of third place is that it reifies a place for human to interact in sincere and authentic ways, and to do so entirely at their whim. They entered this space whenever they wanted, without hindrance and with full knowledge that they were always welcome. Always. We are confronted with this truth: "God is the space that takes place between two people talking." (I believe this is from *When Bad Things Happen to Good People* by Harold Kushner, but I am not certain).

The family table cannot be easily replicated.

Am I fetishizing this table? Probably, but for a good reason: It's a necessary salve in a society where such places rapidly disappear. How many times have my wife and I lamented the passing of the Conti for this very reason: There is no longer a family table to go to and we've not found a place to replicate it since. Something about the human psyche suggests we need such sites of engagement, and when we don't have them, we miss them deeply, or nostalgize about their ability to bring a smile to our faces and now must search for this cheer elsewhere. As society increasingly accepts food delivery rather than dining out, the family table may go the way of the horse and buggy as important forms of transportation. And then our identity formation must happen elsewhere, if it happens at all.

Third place restaurants remind us how much we need human interaction, how vital it is to the conduct of human affairs. The world may be more efficient when it goes to food delivery, but the intangible of the family table is lost, and one more tiny aspect of our humanity in the burgeoning technological space vanishes, never to return. That cannot be a world we should want. I believe strongly in technology, but it should never come at the expense of our humanity.

On the last day of the Continental, there were many tears shed because everyone gathered knew an era had ended. As the hours ticked by, no one needed a reminder of how special this was. All the family members were gathered, including spouses, and this last shift was the last piece of the painting. And once completed, it would be given to all those who were lucky to witness it and to take into their hearts. Just like poetry does. I am not sure, even looking back on that precious day, what I really felt, or if I could fully describe the emotion. Not sadness, or regret, or joy that my life would no longer be tethered to the restaurant and the obligations I had to it. Instead, a kind of strange calmness came over me, because deep down I long ago foresaw that the restaurant could not be sustained. We were old and increasingly felt like dinosaurs in a world ruled by speed and efficiency. In fact, we probably lasted longer than I had expected; the point here is not about the length of time but accepting that the end was to come was already familiar to me. And now that it was coming, I was mixed about whether this was a good thing or bad. In time, I would see that a large part of my life would go missing and not be filled or replaced by anything else. I knew that the Conti was not merely a chapter in my life, but it had strangely become my life, even if I never regarded it as such. Only now, when it has ceased, can I see that that day was a funeral for a way of life that once passed, passed forever. Like the village we left behind, which itself is more or less dormant, the restaurant had passed away, like a human being. And that final day was the burial service. Only when the last customer had left and the lights were turned off could we silently cry for the passing of an age.

And who were our regulars and those folks at the family table? There was Russell Valley, who ran a landscaping business, seemingly from the restaurant. He spent hours there every day, so it became obvious to us that the Conti was his office. He brought in his only employee,

Keith, on occasion, and they discussed projects, and he took care of the bookkeeping. It reminded me of the times where eateries served in this same capacity, an office for businesspeople, or even in the early modern era as proto stock exchanges.

Russell was probably the finest soul I've ever met. If we ask the question: "Who among us is the best at being a human being?" then surely for me, none matched Russell. He was kind, considerate, cheerful, always optimistic, and low-key. His politics tended to grate on the more progressives at the table, but they were never extreme or polemical. He sided with George W. Bush's invasion of Iraq and Afghanistan after the tragedy of 9/11. But he also celebrated Barack Obama's presidential victory in 2008. And he was the best soccer player I've ever played against, slow but sure-footed and deceptively great on the ball. I hated him for it; now I appreciate his skills since I can no longer play.

But as a friend, supporter, thoughtful giver, and honest gentleman, he was exemplary. Along with my brother, he was my greatest booster during my difficult graduate school days, when each week I declared I would quit. Patiently and with humor, he counseled me against it. Over and over again. Dozens of times? Perhaps more. My emotions are telegraphed, so he knew the moment I walked in the door what my mood was like. And he took action. When I started a sort of small cinema at Bulldog News, showing a film on DVD there on Friday nights, he was there to help me arrange and break down the chairs afterwards. For all my ups and downs, he was there. No better friend could I have had. He was a gift of the Continental as well.

Our lives need a Russell Valley in them. We need a voice that brings us down from our pompous dreams and lifts us from our broken hearts. We need someone to puncture through the fables of existence, but also one who reminds us of what is valuable and necessary in building a decent life: good friends, good conversation, good food, good memories. It reminds me of a quip I once heard: When I was twenty, I wanted to change the world; when I got to forty, I just wanted to avoid scandal. To that I can add, at sixty, I want to be surrounded by great friends.

Then there was Calhoun. Well into his sixties, he began coming to the restaurant usually around 9:30 or 10 p.m., when the kitchen was near to or actually closing. Yet, we always accommodated him for his favorite meal: a slab of salmon atop a warm pita with tartar sauce and a glass of red wine. And then for the next hour or so he regaled us with his vast knowledge of politics, Southern culture (he was from Raymond, Mississippi), and about cooperatives (he volunteered at PCC Community

Markets) and commented on the news. His eruditeness astonished me; his encyclopedic mind of American politics truly was breath-taking. He held us in awe at what he knew, what he recalled. He also specialized in ancient Greek and Roman history and knew his Plato from his Lucretius. And he was progressive. A white Southern progressive. Those hours I spent with him were like listening to brilliant lectures. And, like Russell, he was cheerful and optimistic. Never critical of anyone, except the crooked and the corrupt, he astonished his listeners with his analysis. And at the end of each conversation, often near midnight, when it was time to go home, when he had finished his second glass of red wine, he'd rise from his chair, satisfied at the food and conversation, smile in his friendly way, and utter, "Tomorrow's another exciting day!"

When he passed away, we mourned. I attended a service at Green Lake, near his beloved Green Lake PCC where he spent so many hours helping customers to their cars or gathering carts. And smiling, always smiling. Can Uber Eats provide the same humanity? Can we find souls like Calhoun's anyone else but at third places? *It's a Wonderful Life's* George Bailey was right: We are rich when we have friends. Not just individually, but as a community; the community is richer when there are good friends in it. My life is now poorer that Calhoun and Russell are no longer in it (Russell passed away some years later after a long illness, and it was friends that stepped in to help him, including my brother, Demetre).

Tomorrow's another exciting day.

CHAPTER TEN

The Check, Please

Or is it?

Will tomorrow be another exciting day for third place restaurants? What happens to our lives when such community spots vanish or die? For a time, I clipped *New York Times* articles about the passing of third place operations, not just restaurants, but community barbershops, hardware stores, record shops, hair salons, and the like. On the one hand, it's apparently part of the creative destruction of capitalism; the idea being old businesses that cannot survive new conditions must die to make room for new operations better suited to the new environment. At one time, the Conti was part of the new environment when it opened its doors in 1968. By 2013, when there were fewer Greek restaurants across the nation, they had joined the old and passé.

The main thesis of this book suggests third places like the Continental educated the immigrant families that owned them in American society. If such places vanish, are there substitutes to carry on this function? I mentioned previously in the restaurant world the appearance of different types of cuisines, reflecting immigration from Africa and the Caribbean. The Americanization process continues there and will persist, but it may not do so quite in the same way. Today, restaurants face huge pressures that my family did not face. The move to delivery opens up new revenue streams but also dining into a radical new experience. When it is easier to order out and have the meal delivered, the capacity to sustain third places is lost. There is little incentive to put community over convenience. It is simply easier to order out and have the food delivered to your home (house, apartment, etc.) than it is to drive to a place, particularly if it is far away. It's a fact that third places require our souls be engaged. It is much easier to stay at home and have the food come there. No need to dress or put on our public face to make the trip possible. Yet, in doing so, we lose the nurturing aspects of third places I've outlined in this book. On balance, we lose more (in our humanity) than we gain (in convenience). It is a tradeoff that in the sum of individual decisions says much about the state of our civilization today.

When I conducted my dissertation research in the village during a miserably hot summer, I grew to appreciate the value of the *kafenia* there for how they sustained community life. It was never apparent before, but it became crystal clear that summer. I was both excited and unnerved by my discovery. In pre-television days, the village café was the center of most social life in the community, which, like the village church, brought people together who did not often like each other. My grandmother hated her neighborhood of retirees, yet they were found praying in the same church in the village. When this ceases, it is no small wonder that tribalism rises and political divisions flourish.

I came back after that summer excited by what I discovered. It was both exciting to me as a budding social scientist, but it also reaffirmed the value of the Conti for me in a way that I had not really noticed before. It was the start of rethinking what it meant to be part of a third place for the local community. It was the beginning of an appreciation of the institutional importance of communal existence for me that found full expression in these pages. Most cultural markers today announce and promote our individuality. Many of these are myths. We are the products of our surroundings, and most of those involve institutions of one kind or another: families, schools, places of worship, work environments. Please tell me if any of these institutions promote our socialization or our individuality more. Does rooting for your favorite football club promote your individuality or your social identity? When you play Minecraft do you do so because you can be alone or because you know millions of others are doing the same?

The basis for Western democracy began in the marketplace of ancient Athens. In the "agora," people shopped, ran into each other to gossip, but also encountered one another in political discussions. This was common in the ancient world (we tend to assume Western civilization began with classical Athens, when she borrowed so much from the Middle East), but the Greeks took this practice to new levels. Athenians met in the agora as social creatures; the pleasant weather certainly encouraged this kind of activity, but so did the nature of the city as a polyglot mixture of natives and immigrants (and slaves). From this developed the assembly, or "ecclesia" (the same word for today's church in modern Greek), that ushered in parliaments and congress. Ancient Greeks insisted on social activity; Athens donated theater tickets to those who could not afford them so that they could join theatrical performances, the equivalent today of the city of Seattle handing out movie tickets to the disadvantaged.

What happens when the world collapses it in itself and we live out our lives as individuals? We need not speculate; this happened with the Covid-19 pandemic. We all saw what life looks like when we are barricaded at home, unable to engage with the community except via Skype or Zoom. Throughout the pandemic I kept thinking about the Conti or about my favorite little taverna in downtown Athens. These images came to mind because my soul yearned for them. I wanted and needed to be with people again, to sit in the little eatery next to Syngrou Fix metro station, people watch, read my newspaper, and enjoy the pleasant weather. I grew to detest the compartmentalization of life under the pandemic.

In writing these words, I may be suffering too much making a plea for appreciating the value of third places. In another world, I need not make such an appeal; the power of third places would be obvious to all. The fact that I do so suggests this message is not clear to everyone and why my pleas must be made. The *kafenia* that first appeared in the United States provided Greek immigrants with a familiar place that provided comfort and warmth in a strange culture. They also gave expression to their understanding of how the world operated, where one's social skills helped secure jobs, places to live, and suitable partners. It was a valuable community service they provided, and more or less free of charge (or for the price of a cup of Greek/Turkish coffee). What would have society looked like, at least for Greek Americans, if *kafenia* had not existed? Consider the moments in your life when you were helped by someone and their impact on your course of your life.

For restaurants, it takes very little to become a third place.

No one came into the Conti because of its décor, although we were unique in offering two skylights that on winter days provided much needed exposure to the sun for those customers who needed it for their mental health. Otherwise, it was a nondescript place. For much of its history, it had the look of an East Coast diner—spinning outdoor sign fashionable in the 1950s, indoor plants in the main dining area alongside the front windows, and a small incline upon entry (the door was located in the middle of the frontage, and always felt as if you were walking into an old apartment building). Once inside, to your immediate left was the cash register. Ahead, two spaces—to the right the "pastry side" as we called it, and to the left, the main dining area indicated by the carpet on the floor. On the pastry side, along a wall were shelves of groceries and Greek tourist items—vases, ancient plates, and other kitsch. We even

A key attraction for some customers was the skylight above the dining area. During the dark winter months, just having some light, or rain tapping, above while waiting could be soothing.

sold Greek fishermen's hats. At the rear of the pastry side were two display cases—one refrigerated for cakes (Greek walnut cakes and the like) and the other plain (for showcasing cookies, baklava, and typically Greek pastries like apple dumplings and raisin bars). To go to the bathroom, one walked to behind the pastry counters and up to a "T"—to the left were the restrooms and to the right, along a short but very narrow corridor, was the office. If I had a nickel for every time a customer headed to the office, I'd be quite rich. For much of the Conti's life, the family table was located next to the refrigerated pastry counter.

It did not require an architect to note that the place had an "added-on" quality. The pastry side was the original operation ("The Continental Pastry Shop") before it expanded to take the adjacent space. A dining room was added, along with the bathrooms, the server area, the kitchen, and in the back, the prep kitchen that also included the original baking oven—a big monster that in the later years often broke down and where my father spent hundreds of hours inside it (he managed, despite his girth, to crawl inside and conduct repairs— miraculously, he always managed to fix it!). Completing the tour, the back of the restaurant was shelving with supplies, and in later years, two large refrigerators for storage. The very, very back had a changing room and a bathroom. There was also a rear door to the place, that when opened brought you to the rear parking space. But it was not level, so on many occasions, the drain just outside the door would fill, and water flooded our floor. I do not have many fond memories of such events.

The expansion brought a dining area that resembled a subterranean storage space. The twenty-one tables were terribly crowded together, and it was always a wonder to me how people could eat with other patrons just inches away. Was it a kind of social game to see how to maintain a conversation when folks next to you were doing the same? To this day, I do not know the answer. What I do know is this would not be my first dining choice going out. Up until 2000, the restaurant, like all others, allowed smoking. It's scarcely possible to envision this, but it's a historical fact if you care to ignore me. Prior to this, my brother decided to create a non-smoking section in the main dining area, an attempt to go along with the changing times and not entirely unique to our restaurant (similar to non-smoking sections in airplanes). Of course, the cigarette smoke wafted into the non-smoking area, immediately invalidating it. I admire his effort but eventually he gave it up when one day, January 2, 2000, to be precise, my sister took a piece of paper and a felt marker, scribbled "Now Non-Smoking" and promptly taped it to the front door. And that is how the restaurant became non-smoking before city ordinances made it permanent.

It was not merely the packed-sardines quality of the dining room, but being next to the server area the recipient of the noise emanating from it. Servers preparing food and drink cause noise, as does dropping dirty dishes on the metal tray in the server area that led to the dishwasher behind the partitioning wall. Yet, there was one advantage: the easily moved tables meant that for large groups could easily be accommodated. And they were; large groups don't mind the server area noise, they dominated the conversations and felt cozy in the space. That is why we attracted so many large groups.

The pathway from the dining area through the server area to the kitchen when we first took over the restaurant in 1974 ran smack through the cooking area—and this is where I worked for several years in the haze and bustle of weekend mornings, the busiest shifts of the week. To the right were the grills and to the left was the table where we assembled the plates. Imagine cooking for one hundred customers with servers and others constantly walking between grills and tables. It was a mess because the kitchen was added on when the pastry shop expanded.

All of it was housed in a building that dated from the 1920s that was built simply and quickly. The main frames were cement blocks that did little to keep the heat in during winter and the heat out during summer. We baked and froze in equal measure, and it was a matter of picking your poison. The aging building meant all kinds of critters walked and crawled around the space; cockroaches were always the problem and occasionally mice that had to be dealt with. Once a small mouse got loose in the dining area and my quick-thinking sister smashed it with her foot and swept it away in a hurry.

This was the Conti. Nobody's front cover candidate for *Gourmet* magazine.

There was a major kitchen remodel in the late 1970s, and one for the main dining area two decades later. The kitchen gave cooks their own exclusive space, and the dining area upgrade made the space more inviting and less cluttered. But the family table remained. The family remained. And so did the customers. They had their own families, and we watched as their kids grew, and soon two generations of customers were coming to the Conti. A sense of continuity quickly developed. My father dispensed a lot of candy and cookies to growing kids, and in time the kids' kids were treated to the sweets, and on it went. The circle of life.

The wonderful documentary *Streit's: Matzo and the American Dream* captures this golden circle and the challenge in maintaining a third place. It tells of a matzo factory in Manhattan's Lower East Side and its legacy in a Jewish neighborhood.[1] The factory was founded early in the twentieth century, but as the neighborhood gentrified, it became a beached whale, out of sorts in the community that once sustained it. Historian Elissa Sampson could be speaking about the Conti and its struggles to maintain the old in an increasingly corporate environment: "Staying in place is really the battle about belonging and diversity. Once that diversity is gone, it becomes homogenous. It becomes just another franchise. It becomes another superstore. That sense of belonging is extremely important. Losing a sense of belonging, it disassociates you from everything."[2] The loss of belonging resulted in many of our regulars feeling abandoned and bereft, which explains why the sadness and anger over the Conti closing remained (and perhaps still does amongst its many aficionados) as a singular tragedy. In a rapidly changing culture, continuity is important.

Because food creates its own sense of identity and evokes memory, it takes on a life of its own. "A place like Streit's has to evoke nostalgia in people, since that's what the building speaks to," Sampson continues. "The olfactory, the food, the alimentary, all these things go together. We're not outside of our bodies, right? Our memories connect to food and to smell and to the sensory, in every sense. How could I not see the nineteenth century in a place like this? But I can tell you the fact that the Streit family has managed to survive on Suffolk Street is nothing other than extraordinary."[3] (Eventually the Streit owners decided to move the factory from Manhattan to the suburbs.) For those kids who grew up in the Conti, this association of food to the memory of my father handing them sweets somehow registered, since they grew and returned with their own children. Like salmon returning to the spawning grounds, this may be a primal action. Certainly, it captures the dilemma many immigrants feel about their homeland and the pain of leaving it.

Sampson understands that families are often behind third places, in the widest definition of the term. "When I take people to Streit's, I strongly encourage them to think through what it means for a family to stay in the neighborhood and to make that commitment, and what it means to the community to have that commitment. But it's their choice. It's Aron's family, it's his business, and now his desk. And that's a very … that's a real dilemma." We faced this difficult choice of what to do with the Conti when it became obvious we could no longer sustain it. Attempts to find other families to take it over were not successful. So, we were faced with a choice, the choice the Streit's owner faced. In Sampson's own words when the decision was made:

It's a loss. It's what it evoked. It was the taste, but the sense of persistence and continuity, and it was one of those few things that was still there. By the time they actually made their announcement, people knew that the ovens were getting harder to maintain. And that they're going up against both very big manufacturers and a conglomerate, and they understood that the family was between a rock and a hard place. What was very clear to me was there was no criticism of the family. People knew what was involved, which is that they had really tried hard under difficult circumstances, and what most people wanted was the city to intervene and offer them some incentives to stay because of the workers and because of the importance of Streit's in anchoring the last of the Lower East Side's manufacturing as well as part of its Jewish identity. New Yorkers want to have a sense of belonging to place. Streit's was part of that. [On video, one of the owners, Aron Yagoda, lovingly taps a wall of the now empty building]. Having said that, the most important thing is that they decided to keep on with the brand and the manufacturing.[4]

We did not. When we closed the doors on the fateful last day in June in 2013, the Conti entered history. The Conti had become another story. And yet the forty years we left behind did have an impact. Sampson summarizes it well: "Like everything, you can read stories in many, many different ways, but this story should be read as one of perseverance, and loyalty to a neighborhood. And then, at the point where the neighborhood itself is no longer recognizable, the family gets to reposition itself to keep the business going. So, it's a narrative of sorts, with stages. But that middle stage of staying in the Lower East Side for five generations is a very precious one, and one that people will not forget."[5]

And that is certainly what happened with the Conti.

Conclusion

White ethnicity was the process by which immigrants like my family became "white." In the color rainbow that is America, we took on this hue against the backdrop of more "colored" folks—namely, African Americans, Asian Americans and Native Americans. Had they not existed it might have proved difficult to become as white as we did. That is the theory and certainly at the turn of the twentieth century, that was the case. In the twenty-first century, even as racial politics return, the reality is more complicated. Does my family feel "white"? What exactly is whiteness and is its meaning? Do we really still care about such labels? Are they necessary to describe our experiences in the United States?

We came as foreigners and we struggled to integrate, the same as I am sure an American family would have had had they moved to Greece. Leaving behind the familiar is never easy, and adapting to new surroundings is not always easy or even rewarding. At first. Only after years of intense struggle do the fruits of this work reveal themselves and only with great modesty. We relate to others as human beings, so in time the immigrant feels a small tug of connection with other ordinary people; together, they signal the start of integration. I felt that most assuredly when I began working at the restaurant; it did what my school, my friendships, my family failed to do, and that is to absorb me into the greater society.

And I did not have to do anything particularly special. It was a gift that came with simply doing my work and my duties. I became a restaurant man, not by choice, and in doing so I reveled in the struggle of hard work, patience, professionalism, determination and problem-solving. The external world often places hierarchies or categories in what we do, who we are, but in the main, work is a great leveler. Either you work hard, or you do not. And therefore, the patina of difference that sets apart the immigrant from the native disappears, and I was left with the camaraderie of the moment. My coworker is in the same boat as me, and we row together in one direction. In such moments I forgot that I was an immigrant but became a member of a team. I lost my past as an immigrant; what does the past matter when a job must be done?

This does not mean that white ethnicity has no validity. The term came about to describe a condition, not unique to the United States, but certainly exposed and explored and heightened in this country like in few others with its vaunted history of immigration, that saw the dividing line between citizen and alien. It became a way to judge others: differences between the native and the foreigner could not be bridged, and therefore were set in stone. No matter how successful the immigrant, there would always be something to set him apart. And white ethnicity did that skillfully, unfairly, cruelly, and, most especially, racially.

Immigrant-ness is a state of mind, not a condition of the body or the soul. It is not a disease, or an illness to be treated, but rather simply a perception of the world. Over time it can change, and over time the immigrant can become native, as we have witnessed many times in the nation's history; the "black" Irish who came as unwanted immigrants in the mid–1800s themselves later become nativists and unwelcoming of Slavs and Jews in the early 1900s. Greeks who faced discrimination in the United States in the 1960s retired to Greece and regarded the Syrian refugees with hostility and anger. It is a never-ending cycle, one that increases in intensity as the world's population shifts from war, climate change, economic ruin, or megalomania.

I have never considered myself an ethnic white because I feel the label misrepresents as much as it explains. It tells me that I am not and cannot be part of the dominant culture of the country, as if that culture can define who and what I am. What defines me are my actions, and what I have done in my work life. The Conti became a central part of my identity, which has steadfastly remained, because it became a lens to the world. It trained me to view reality from the vantage point of honorable if difficult work, but one where I felt the satisfaction of a job accomplished, of a task completed, of a customer's hunger quelled. I took pride in that; where is the white ethnicity?

"You cooked for the dominant group," comes the reply, "who did not honor you as much as you catered to their needs. White ethnicity is about imbalance, you are the servant, and the mostly-white customer is your master." So as much as I took pride in providing a valuable service to customers, which they paid for, no matter the freedom of exchange provided, or the informal contractual obligation fulfilled, the reality I am told is that the relationship is asymmetrical. Cooking, long usually done by women in society for as long as humans have existed, is not a profession, but a duty. Its feminine association denigrates its social status; a cook is a glorified servant who works under harsh conditions for abysmally low wages.

Was I blind to this reality when I cooked at the Conti? If so, why? The struggle here is to balance two contrarian viewpoints that seemingly have little ground for compromise. Perhaps I was too young to see the full effects of my work, to understand it within the larger context of societal interactions. In the micro world there is little to paint cooking and restaurant work in ethno-racial terms, but as one rises to the macro level, to the state where patterns are more visible, white ethnicity emerges in stark terms. The preponderance of ethnic restaurants and the preponderance of white customers is an unmistakable fact. For many Americans, introduction to another ethnic culture is through its cuisine. Is there confusion between white ethnicity and the exoticization of food?

The real issue is not one between white ethnicity and exotic food, but the Western divide between the mind and the body. One of the most compelling arguments in Ray's *Ethnic Restaurateur* book is the premise that in Western society we not only divide the mind and the body, but we place more important on the mind than the body. This division is a key feature of Western civilization, and part of Ray's mission, as well as other academics, is to bring food—as a sustainer of the body—into a greater balance with the mind. In the Western model, the body is the receptacle of the mind, but it is also the dirtier of the two. Hence elements associated with the body are downgraded whereas thought and the mind are pure, direct, unsullied by smell, taste, excrement, and the like.

Restaurants, by virtue of feeding the body, thus can seem to many as unequal to more intellectual pursuits. This, then, is the rub with white ethnicity; it relates that Anglo-Americans investigate higher creative pursuits while immigrants, being typically less educated, pursue more utilitarian activities. The only place where these two opposing sides can meet is through food, but once there, there is an unequal exchange and once the exchange is over, once the meal has been ordered, delivered, and paid for, there is little further contact between the parties. The transaction ends there. There is nothing more to transact.

What I can offer this debate is that while this may be the case many times, at the Conti the result I feel was radically different. Perhaps special neighborhood places like the Conti (as a "mediating commons")

140

negate the features of white ethnicity and transcend its narrow-minded limitations. This is not an argument based on hard scientific data, but on personal and perhaps even anecdotal evidence, so much caution is advised. Perhaps other ethnic restaurateurs will step forward with their own experiences to buttress or disprove my contention.

Does the growing popularity of ethnic food also negate or minimize the polarizing effects of white ethnicity? Ray suggests that ethnic food follows a hierarchy, yet one that is not entirely suggestive of white ethnicity at work. Italian, Japanese and most certainly French cooking each has evolved into "haute cuisine," while others—notably Chinese, Mexican, and Soul Food—remain down-market.[1] Greek cuisine is somewhere in the middle, with some strides made towards lifting it to higher status. There are several elements that determine how one particular cuisine becomes more "haute" than another, and much of it is determined by the particular ecology of the restaurant marketplace—not only the restaurants and their chefs/owners that lend it such credibility, but so too the food writers and critics in publications like the *New York Times* and *Gourmet* magazine, as well as various television, cable and internet features, and websites.

To make a claim for white ethnicity's racialized and hierarchical reality in regard to ethnic restaurants is to also posit that it extends its influence into the marketplace. But that is difficult to quantify. I know of no study that makes such a claim, nor that backs it up with hard (i.e., interviews, surveys, etc.) evidence. The hierarchies that exist in the ethnic cuisine circle may be less due to any particular effect of white ethnicity (that organizes ethnic groups in the United States according to their utility to the dominant Anglo-American group) and more to the reality of the restaurant marketplace—as one where cuisines go up and down based on changing tastes, the fortunes of specific restaurants, publicity elements, and other ephemeral factors.

So, what happened to my family after the restaurant was sold? As happens to many newly retired folks, it was a hard adjustment. My mother continued to be active, volunteering at the local Greek Orthodox church, but my father—less mobile—spent many of his waking hours in front of the TV set. His bad knees and other various ailments curtailed his mobility, and he found his escape in watching too many sports matches. He didn't like basketball, so he stuck to football and soccer, more the former than the latter.

My brother went to other activities, notably real estate, while still keeping his hand in the restaurant business (at another Greek restaurant as a waiter), and my sister never looked back as she gained stature in her academic career. With the restaurant now closed, or at least, in different hands with a different food concept, I felt both liberated but also chained to its memory. It seems wherever I went there was a former customer to remind me, to ask me, to chide me for closing the place, or to reminisce. It was not easy, confronting these folks on a regular basis; it was like having the same nightmare over and over again.

We all had to adjust to our new lives. My mother perhaps had the easiest time of it, since her cheerful attitude let her accept any new twist that life threw at her with equanimity and grace. As much as friends encouraged me to open up another Conti, I knew that I was not meant for the restaurant business. I could dream, but that is as far as the thought travelled.

Many former customers clamored for my father to publish his recipes. One day he handed me the notes that contained them and asked me to publish

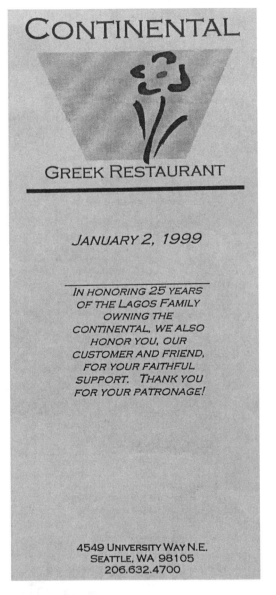

CONTINENTAL

GREEK RESTAURANT

JANUARY 2, 1999

IN HONORING 25 YEARS OF THE LAGOS FAMILY OWNING THE CONTINENTAL, WE ALSO HONOR YOU, OUR CUSTOMER AND FRIEND, FOR YOUR FAITHFUL SUPPORT. THANK YOU FOR YOUR PATRONAGE!

4549 UNIVERSITY WAY N.E.
SEATTLE, WA 98105
206.632.4700

On the 25th anniversary of the restaurant, the family celebrated by rolling back prices to its first year of ownership (1974). Within a few hours, thanks to cell phones, the place was packed until evening, when the food ran out.

Conclusion

them as a book. I didn't want to add yet another cookbook to a crowded world, so decided to end this book by including the recipes. It seemed a fitting way to close the forty-year chapter in our lives. I also include the recipe for "Taso's Breakfast" and "Helen's Pita" that some folks enjoyed. I did too.

Appendix:
Special Continental Dishes

Owning a restaurant meant we could design our own dishes. Over the years, I developed some interesting ones that involved combining existing foods into new creations (at least they were to me; perhaps they were already created by others). I'll start first with one my mother made that eventually became known as "Helen's Pita." I noticed that my mother loved warming up pita bread and throwing various things on it; it was a quick and easy meal. So, one day I thought, "Why not put some scrambled eggs on a pita, sprinkle it with some feta and top it with a few tomato slices?" I convinced my father to put it on the menu and was surprised that he allowed me to do so. That became a popular breakfast dish: quick, filling and not very expensive.

A second one was called "Jacque's Pita," named after one of our most loyal customers and a true community progressive. Like the other regulars, she is missed. Her pita was simpler than my mother's, and one that she genuinely created: warm pita, with sprinkled feta, olives, and a few sliced tomatoes. Again, quick, filling and cheap. For many years, I had an ambitious desire to create a stand that served a variety of dishes based on pita bread. It never came to fruition. The beauty of both "Helen's Pita" and "Jacque's Pita" was that they are easily made and can be eaten at any time of the day. Eggs are no longer just for breakfast.

When I came to eat at the restaurant in breaks in my academic work or teaching, I had little time to eat. If the restaurant was busy, I had even less time, often gulping down food in between busing tables, taking bills at the cash register, and putting customer orders in the kitchen. So, I developed the habit of putting together meals that did not need cooking, but were already made: lentil soup, warm rice, mixed lettuce, feta cheese. I started with a base, whether it was mixed salad or a bed of steamed rice. With mixed salad, I always threw some rice in and sprinkled feta on top. Sometimes, I even grated a hard-boiled egg on top of

145

this concoction. If I began with a bed of rice, then I spooned warm lentil soup (it's thick, so it goes nicely with the rice) over the top, sprinkled on feta, and enjoyed a delicious and nutritious meal. If I was still hungry, I'd go back for seconds. A variation on this dish involved starting first with a bowl of lentil soup, rather than rice, and putting rice and sprinkled cheese on top (it's a great winter dish).

My favorite meal of all involved some cooking. I love scrambled eggs, and always thought of creative ways to embellish them. When the restaurant was not busy and I could go behind the grill, I'd lay down a bed of rice on a plate, then scramble two eggs and cook a handful of fresh sliced mushrooms on the grill. Once the eggs were thoroughly scrambled, I'd scoop them on top of the rice. When the mushrooms were cooked, I placed them on top of the eggs, then sprinkled on cheese, three slices of tomatoes, and for the embellishment an olive on top of the mound. That became "Taso's Breakfast," and my proudest creation. I was happy when the family consented to include it on the menu.

I had other ideas, too, but they never made it to the menu. I envisioned a variation of Helen's Pita that involved including sliced "Loukanico" Greek sausage (cooked) on top of the scrambled eggs. Adding meat not only gave more protein to the combination, but a good hearty taste. My father made our own Loukanico at the restaurant, without any preservatives, and it was popular with customers. We also made our own pesto, which was far better than any available commercially. Our egg mixture was our own as well. I was proud that my father changed the recipe from the one we inherited from the previous partners, who diluted the egg mix with milk. My father stopped doing that, and the omelettes instantly became better as a result.

I never appreciated what a treat it was for me to exercise my creativity in the kitchen, and how the operation benefited. It had little to do with glory, but with the fact that I could exercise my imagination. Perhaps my true career lay as a cook rather than as an educator. Nevertheless, it was fun to come up with new dishes. I'd eat them over time and eventually other employees began ordering them for their breaks. Soon enough they found their way onto the menu. Did I have any strikes? No one seemed to like my salads with rice and grated hardboiled eggs like I did; that never got on the menu. Likewise for the lentil, rice and feta cheese creation; perhaps it was an acquired taste. I also made a fruit salad: mixed fruit (white grapes, apples, peaches, nectarines, or other preferred fruit), Greek yogurt, ground walnuts, and honey mixed together. That was too time consuming, so it remained a personal favorite only.

With the closing of the restaurant, I no longer exercise my creative cooking spirit. Occasionally I make something at home—the fruit salad is a favorite—but it's rare. With raising a spunky daughter, I no longer have the time to experiment. My creativity had to find other outlets, like writing books.

And, finally, here are my dad's compiled recipes from the restaurant. Enjoy.

Appetizers

Corned Beef Scramble

- 1 large tomato
- 1 bell pepper
- 1 small onion
- olive oil for frying pan
- 1 lb corned beef, cooked
- 15 eggs
- salt and pepper
- 1 sprig of mint leaves

Peel and chop the tomato. Chop the bell pepper. Slice the onion very thin. Heat olive oil in a frying pan and sauté the tomato, bell pepper and onion until very soft. Chop the corned beef into small pieces and add to the frying pan for five minutes, stirring occasionally. Add eggs, salt and pepper to taste and mint leaves and cook until eggs are set.

Makes 5 servings

Chef's Favorite Omelet

- 1 medium tomato
- ¼ lb crumbled feta cheese
- olive oil for skillet
- 3 eggs, beaten
- salt and pepper to taste

Peel and chop the tomato. Heat olive oil in a frying pan and sauté the tomato until very soft and liquid is reduced. Add the feta cheese and cook for two minutes. Transfer to a plate and keep warm. Add eggs and salt and pepper to the skillet and cook until eggs are cooked on the bottom. Add tomato and feta to center third of eggs. Fold each side over the center to form an omelet. Turn omelet over, cooking both sides, until center of omelet is cooked through.

Makes 1 serving

Feta Cheese Omelet

- 3 eggs, beaten
- ¼ lb shredded feta cheese
- olive oil for frying pan
- salt and pepper

Heat oil and add beaten eggs to the pan, adding salt and pepper to taste. Sprinkle the feta cheese over the center third of the eggs. When the bottom of the eggs are cooked, fold each side over the center to form the omelet, cooking on both sides until the center of the omelet is cooked through. Serve with toast and fries.

Makes 1 serving

Mushroom, Onion and
Bell Pepper Omelet

- ½ cup mushrooms, chopped
- ½ cup onions, chopped
- ½ cup bell pepper, chopped
- 4 eggs, beaten
- olive oil for skillet

Heat oil in a skillet. Add the mushrooms, onions, and bell pepper and sauté until slightly soft. Transfer to a plate and keep warm. Add egg mixture to the skillet, adding salt and pepper to taste. When the bottom of the eggs are cooked, add the vegetables to the center third of the eggs and fold each side over the center, forming the omelet. Cook omelet on both sides until center of omelet is cooked through. Serve with toast and fries.

Makes 2 servings

Souvlaki and Eggs

- ½–1 lb beef flap meat (or similar cut) or chicken
- 1 large onion
- 1–2 bell peppers
- eggs, quantity as needed

Cut meat and vegetables into bite-sized pieces and place on skewers. Broil as desired and serve with eggs of choice and Greek fries.

Dolmathes

- 1 gallon rice
- ¾ gallon water
- 3 lbs minced onions
- 3 oz salt

- 10 lbs ground lamb
- 24 oz tomato puree
- 1 oz black pepper
- 1 oz ground anise
- fresh mint, chopped fine or 1 cup dried
- pickled grape leaves

Sauté onions until soft. Add lamb and spices and cook for a few minutes. Add tomato puree. Stir to blend. Add water and bring to a boil. Add rice; stir well and cook on high heat until water is absorbed, stirring continuously. Remove from heat and allow to cool.

To prepare and stuff grape leaves:

Carefully separate grape leaves and rinse. Spoon approximately ¼ cup of the rice mixture onto the center of each grape leaf and roll tightly. Adjust amount of filling to the size of the grape leaf. Layer dolmathes in a stock pot or deep skillet, adding enough water to barely cover dolmathes. Sprinkle about ¼ cup lemon juice over the dolmathes, cover and simmer approximately 30 minutes. Liquid will be mostly absorbed. Serve with dolmathes sauce.

This amount of filling makes about 600 pieces—6 pieces per serving. Halve this filling recipe for dolmathes sauce.

Dolmathes Sauce

- ½ gallon water
- 2 cups cold water
- 3½ oz cornstarch
- 5 egg yolks
- 1 cup lemon juice
- 1 tsp anise
- 1 tsp salt

Boil the ½ gallon of water and remove from heat. In a separate large bowl, combine the two cups cold water with cornstarch and mix thoroughly. Add the ½ gallon of hot water to the cornstarch mixture and stir to combine. Add the egg yolks one at a time, mixing well after each addition. Stir in lemon juice, anise and salt. Stir and cook until thickened.

Makes a little over ½ gallon—enough sauce for about 300 dolmathes.

Taramosalata

- 8 large potatoes (bakers)
- 1 jar tarama (approx 1 lb)
- 1 bottle lemon juice (approx 16 oz)
- water as necessary
- olive oil as necessary

Boil, peel and mash the potatoes. Stir in the tarama and lemon juice. Add olive oil to mixture until combined. If too thick, add water as necessary. Mixture should be similar to soft set pudding. Serve with pita bread.

Hummus

- 2 #10 cans of garbanzo beans, drained
- 3 heads of garlic, peeled
- 32 oz jar of tahini
- 64 oz water
- 24 oz olive oil

Blend garbanzo beans and garlic well in a food processor. Transfer to a mixer and add tahini. Mix well. Add olive oil and combine thoroughly. Add water as necessary to obtain desired consistency. Cool and serve with pita bread.

Calamari

- 1 can of calamari (14–16 oz)
- 2 tomatoes, chopped
- 1 large onion, sliced thin
- 1 cup parsley, chopped
- olive oil
- salt and pepper
- 2 cloves garlic, chopped fine

Drain and wash the calamari well and chop into bite sized pieces. Heat the olive oil and sauté the onions until soft. Add tomatoes and parsley and continue to sauté until tomatoes are very soft. Add salt, pepper and calamari and sauté for two to three more minutes. Add the garlic and cook for only about five seconds to preserve the fresh taste.

Makes 3 servings

Melitzanosalata

- 1 #10 can eggplant (baked and ground)
- 2 heads garlic (approx), peeled and smashed
- 32 oz olive oil
- 1 cup red wine vinegar (to taste)
- ¾ oz salt
- ½ oz pepper

Thoroughly combine all ingredients. Refrigerate. May be served chilled or at room temperature. Serve with pita bread.

Makes 9 servings

Tzatziki

- 4 lbs plain yogurt, drained, or 48 oz Kefir yogurt, undrained
- 2 large cucumbers, grated
- 1 oz crushed garlic (or 4–7 large cloves) to taste
- 1 oz salt, to taste
- 1 tsp ground black pepper
- 1 tbsp dill weed
- ¼–⅓ cup lemon juice, to taste
- 1 cup olive oil

Thoroughly squeeze all the water out of the grated cucumber. Combine yogurt, cucumber, garlic, dill weed, lemon juice, salt and pepper in a mixing bowl and mix well while slowly adding the olive oil. Refrigerate for at least an hour before serving to blend flavors.

Skordalia

- 12 to 14 potatoes (Russets)
- 4 heads of garlic, peeled
- ¾ gallon whole milk
- 24 oz olive oil
- 2 oz salt
- 8 oz red wine vinegar, to taste

Boil potatoes. Peel and mash in a bowl. Smash garlic and add to potatoes. Add milk, olive oil, salt, and vinegar and mix well. Serve at room temperature. Serve as a dip with vegetables, pita bread, etc.

Zucchini Fritters

- 1 lb zucchini, coarsely grated
- ½ lb feta cheese, crumbled
- 6 green onions, minced
- ½ cup fresh dill, chopped, or ¼ cup dried, to taste
- ¼ cup fresh parsley, chopped
- 3 eggs, lightly beaten
- 1 cup all purpose flour
- pinch of ground pepper
- oil for frying

Squeeze the zucchini to eliminate water. Combine with the remaining ingredients, shape into patties and pan fry in oil.

Saganaki

- ¾ lb kefalotiri cheese wedge
- lemon

Slice the cheese into ¼ inch slices and fry in olive oil until browned on both sides. Squeeze lemon over cheese.

Salads

Greek Salad

- 2 cups lettuce, chopped
- ¼ cup feta cheese, crumbled
- tomato wedges
- olives
- 2 hard boiled eggs, sliced
- oregano (optional)

Combine ingredients and serve with olive oil and red wine vinegar.

Horiataki Salad

- 2–3 tomatoes, sliced
- 1 cucumber, sliced
- 1 green pepper, sliced
- 1 small onion, sliced
- 8–10 olives
- feta, 1" × 1" cube
- oregano, sprinkled over top

Combine ingredients and serve with olive oil and red wine vinegar dressing.

Spanaki Salad

- 2 cups spinach, chopped
- ¼ cup crumbled feta
- tomato wedges
- olives
- 2 hard boiled eggs, sliced
- oregano (optional)

Toss spinach with rest of ingredients and top with dressing of choice.

Soups

Avgolemono

- 2¼ lbs rice
- 10 oz butter
- 5 oz chicken base
- 1 oz salt
- 3 gallons water
- 20 eggs, separated
- 24 oz lemon juice, to taste

Bring the rice, butter, chicken stock, salt, and water to a boil. Lower heat, cover and simmer until rice is tender. Meanwhile, separate the 20 eggs and place whites in a large bowl. Set aside yolks. Beat the egg whites until stiff. Add yolks one by one while beating the whites. Stir in lemon juice. One ladle at a time, transfer broth from soup very slowly, stirring continuously, into egg mixture. When the egg white bowl is full, pour mixture back into pot with any remaining broth and stir to combine.

Makes 20–25 servings

Faki (Lentil Soup)

- 3 lbs lentils
- 3 lbs chopped onions
- 3 oz salt
- 10–12 bay leaves
- 6 cloves of garlic, sliced
- 3 gallons of water
- ¾ cup tomato puree
- 24 oz olive oil
- 8 oz red wine vinegar

Combine lentils, onions, salt, bay leaves, garlic and water. Bring to boil. Reduce to a simmer and cook until lentils and vegetables are tender. Stir in tomato puree and five minutes later add oil and vinegar. Stir thoroughly to combine flavors.

Makes 20–25 bowls

Fasolatha (White Bean Navy Soup)

- 2 lbs white beans, soaked/ softened
- 2 gallons water
- 2 onions, chopped
- ½ bunch celery, chopped
- 4 carrots, sliced
- 1 cup (approx), tomato puree
- 24 oz olive oil
- 2 red chili peppers, chopped
- 1½ oz salt

Wash and soak white beans the night before. Drain water from beans. In large soup pot over medium high heat add two gallons water, beans, onions, celery, carrots and chili peppers. Bring to soft boil, then turn heat down to simmer. Cover and cook until beans are just tender, stirring occasionally. Add the tomato puree and the olive oil, and salt to taste. Stir to combine.

Makes 16–20 servings

Garbanzo Bean Soup

- 2 lbs raw chicken, cut in bite-size pieces
- #10 can garbanzo beans
- ¼ gallon hot water

- ¼–½ cup olive oil for sautéing
- 1½ lbs onions, chopped
- ½ tsp cumin
- 1 oz salt

Drain garbanzo beans and wash three times with warm water. Drain. In a large skillet, sauté onions and chicken pieces until chicken is browned. Add beans and cumin and stir for a few minutes. Add water and salt and stir. Cook on medium heat for 15–20 minutes until water looks creamy (from bean starch).
Makes 8–10 servings

Pastas, Rice and Sides

Makaronia Horiataka

- pasta
- butter
- mizithra cheese
- garlic, sliced

Cook pasta; drain. Sauté garlic in butter and add to pasta. Mix thoroughly and add mizithra cheese. Serve hot.

Green Beans with Vegetables

- 2 lbs fresh green beans or 96 oz (#10 can) green beans, drained
- 2 ripe tomatoes, chopped large
- 2 potatoes, peeled and chunked
- 2 zucchini, cut in
- fourths lengthwise
- 2 large onions, sliced
- 1 cup water
- 6 garlic cloves, chopped
- 1 tbsp dried dill weed
- salt, pepper to taste
- olive oil for sautéing

Prepare the beans, tomatoes, potatoes, zucchini, onions and garlic. Combine all ingredients in a skillet or Dutch oven and sauté in olive oil. Add water as necessary to prevent sticking.

Mixed Vegetables

- 20 onions, sliced
- 1 bunch celery, chopped
- 2 lbs mushrooms, sliced
- olive oil for sautéing
- 3 oz salt
- 12 bay leaves

154

Combine all ingredients in large stock pot. Sauté on medium until desired tenderness. Serve with meat or fish.

Makes 18–24 servings

Fasolia

- 3 onions, chopped
- 3 potatoes, peeled and chopped
- olive oil for sautéing
- 96 oz (#10 can) green beans, drained, or 2½ lbs fresh green
- beans, cooked
- 2 ripe tomatoes or ½ cup tomato puree
- 3–4 garlic cloves, chopped
- 2 tbsp dill weed
- salt to taste

Sauté the onions and potatoes. Add the can of green beans and tomato puree. (If using fresh green beans, cook first until tender before adding to recipe.) Add salt and dill to taste.

Makes 8–10 servings

Greek Fries

- frozen potato wedges or coins
- salt and pepper
- oregano
- feta (optional)

Deep fry potatoes and drain oil. Sprinkle with salt mixed with black pepper. Sprinkle with oregano and feta if desired.

Greek Rice Pilaf

- 2 gallons hot water
- 3 oz chicken stock or base
- 8½ lbs rice (1 gallon)
- 12 oz butter
- 3 oz salt
- ½ oz thyme leaves

Cook the rice in a pot or rice cooker with all the ingredients until water is absorbed.

Makes 30–35 servings

Rice Sauce

- 2½ gallons water
- 4 lbs ground beef
- 3 lbs chopped onions
- 3 oz salt

- 48 oz tomato puree
- 2 crumbled cinnamon sticks
- 12 whole cloves
- ½ oz ground black pepper
- 13 oz cornstarch

Sauté onions and salt. Add meat and brown. Stir in water. Add tomato puree. Bring to boil. Add pepper, cinnamon and cloves. Stir well. Boil for about 45 minutes (evaporation will cause it to thicken). Mix cornstarch thoroughly with ¼ gallon (four cups) cold water and add to sauce and simmer for about five minutes to thicken. Remove from heat. Serve over rice pilaf.

Spaghetti Sauce

- 4 lbs onions, chopped fine
- 3–4 green peppers, chopped fine
- 1 head garlic, minced
- 12 lbs ground beef
- 3 oz salt
- 1½ oz ground black pepper
- 32 oz tomato puree
- 1 pinch ground cinnamon
- 1 oz dried mint
- 96 oz (¾ gallon) water

Sauté onions, green peppers, and garlic until soft. Add beef and brown. Stir in salt and pepper. Add tomato puree and stir well. Add water and bring to a boil, stirring. Reduce heat, cover and simmer for one and a half hours. Add remaining ingredients to taste. Serve over spaghetti.

Makes 20–24 servings

Pesto

- 2 cups basil leaves
- ½ cup olive oil
- ½ cup Parmesan or Romano cheese
- 3–4 cloves garlic
- 1 tsp salt
- 2 tbsp pine nuts

Put all ingredients in a blender or food processor. Blend or process until it makes a coarse paste. Pour into a jar and repeat process until jar is nearly full. Stir pesto from time to time to remove bubbles. Add a top layer of olive oil and close the lid. This will keep in the refrigerator for over a year. Do not freeze. The flavor improves with age.

Entrees

Keftethes

- 30 lbs ground beef
- 5 lbs onions, minced
- 12 oz salt
- 1½ oz black pepper
- 1 head garlic, chopped fine
- 1 bunch fresh mint, chopped fine
- 50 eggs
- 5 lbs bread crumbs
- 32 oz olive oil

Combine all ingredients. Form into patties, meatballs, or put on skewers. Pan fry or bake.

Bifteki

- 40 lbs ground lamb
- 6 lbs onions, minced
- 10 oz salt
- 1 oz black pepper
- 1 head garlic, chopped fine
- 1 bunch fresh mint, chopped fine
- 40 eggs
- 4 lb bread crumbs

Combine all ingredients. Form into patties and fry or bake.

Falafel

- 1 cup parsley, chopped
- 1 medium onion, chopped
- 5 cloves garlic, chopped
- ¼ cup cilantro, chopped
- 1 lb canned garbanzo beans
- 2 tsp baking soda
- ¼ cup water
- 2–3 tbsp olive oil

Place all ingredients in a food processor adding the garlic and garbanzos last. Mix with the food processor until combined and similar to puree consistency. Mix baking soda with cold water and add to the mixture. Form into balls (adjusting water as necessary to make rolling easy) and deep fry.

Lamb Burger

- 20 lbs ground lamb
- 4 lbs onions, minced
- 1 head garlic, chopped
- 5 oz salt
- 2½ lbs bread crumbs
- 25 eggs
- 2 oz black pepper, ground
- 1 cup dried mint, to taste

Combine all ingredients. Form into patties, or meatballs, flattening slightly. Grill or pan fry and serve with rice and pita bread.

Makes 60 patties

Mousaka

- 5 lbs ground beef
- 4 onions, chopped
- 3 lbs potatoes, peeled, sliced vertically (⅜" slices)
- 8 eggplants, sliced vertically (⅜" slices)
- ½ cup olive oil
- 96 oz (#10 can) diced tomatoes
- 1 head garlic, chopped
- ½ cup dried mint
- salt and pepper

Combine olive oil and chopped onions in a pot and cook until soft. Add the ground beef and cook until browned. Add the diced tomatoes, garlic, mint, salt and pepper to taste. Cook about 35 minutes on medium high heat, stirring as needed. Skim off fat.

In a prepared pan, layer as follows: all the potatoes, half the eggplant, half the ground beef, the remaining eggplant, and the remaining ground beef. Spread bechamel sauce (below) over the layers and bake at 350F for 45 minutes to one hour.

Cream Sauce/Bechamel

- 2¼ cups butter
- 2¼ cups flour
- ¾ gallon hot milk (12 cups)
- 18 eggs, lightly beaten
- 3 cups parmesan cheese
- 3 tsp salt
- ¾ tsp white pepper, to taste
- 3 tsp nutmeg

Melt butter in a large pot, stirring in the flour to make a roux. Add hot milk, stirring continuously. Once thickened, slowly add the eggs, stirring continuously. Add the parmesan cheese, and salt and pepper to taste. Remove from heat and add nutmeg.

Chicken Breasts in Red Sauce

- olive oil for browning
- 10 chicken breasts
- 1 gallon water
- 4 tbsp tomato puree
- 16 whole cloves
- 1 stick cinnamon, crumbled

- pinch black pepper
- pinch dried mint

- salt to taste

Salt the chicken and brown in olive oil in stock pot. Remove chicken from the stock pot and set aside. Add the rest of the ingredients to the stock pot. Bring to boil and boil until sauce is reduced as desired. Add the chicken back in during the last seven to eight minutes of cooking.

Makes 10 servings

Lamb with Lemon Potatoes

- 10 potatoes, peeled and quartered vertically
- 6 oz butter
- 1 cup lemon juice
- 5 lamb shanks
- oil for browning

- ½ gallon water or as needed
- ¾ oz salt
- 1 tsp oregano
- 2 cloves garlic, sliced

Place potatoes in a large greased roasting pan. Salt the potatoes, dot with butter and sprinkle with lemon juice. Set aside. Salt the lamb and brown in olive oil. Rub with oregano and garlic after turning them over to brown on other side. Add water; cover and simmer for 30 minutes. Transfer meat and drippings to covered roasting pan, arranging around potatoes, and bake at 350F for two and a half hours.

Makes 5 servings

Chicken with Peas

- olive oil for browning
- 4 onions, sliced thin
- salt
- 2 tomatoes, chopped

- 3 chickens, cut in quarters
- 7½ pounds green peas (12 oz/serving)

Brown chicken on all sides. Remove from pan. Sauté onions in same pan, add tomatoes and onions and cook until onions are just soft. Add green peas, stirring to combine. Add salt to meat and tomato mixture and transfer all to baking dish. Cover baking dish and bake at 350F degrees for one and a half hours.

Serves 12

Spanikopita

- ½ bunch scallions, chopped
- ½ cup olive oil, for brushing
- ¼ bunch parsley
- 1½ bags spinach (2¼ lb bag)
- 1 lb cottage cheese
- 5 eggs, beaten
- ¼ cup (approx) lemon juice
- 2 tsp dill, to taste
- ½ lb feta cheese, crumbled
- 1 box filo dough

Wilt spinach and thoroughly squeeze spinach to remove liquid. Set aside. Add olive oil and onions to frying pan and sauté scallions until soft. In a large bowl, mix together the scallions, feta, dill, lemon juice and eggs. Add the spinach, cottage cheese and parsley and stir together thoroughly.

Brush pan with olive oil and place four sheets filo dough in bottom of pan, brushing with olive oil. Fold one filo leaf in half the long way and lay along the long side of baking pan, leaving all but one inch draped over the edge of pan. Repeat on the other long side. Do the same with the two short sides except fold the filo leaves the short way. Spoon spinach filling onto the pan; spread and smooth over filo. Fold the filo that is outside into the pan towards the center, on all four sides, covering the filling.

Add three more filo leaves on top and brush with olive oil. Make one long score down the center the long way, being careful not to cut through the filling. Bake at 350F degrees for about 30 minutes. Cut through the filling along the score and cut into six rows the other way to yield 12 pieces.

Serves 12

Chicken Breast with Garbanzo Beans

- 1 #10 can garbanzo beans
- 3 lbs chicken breast, cut into pieces
- 2 lbs onions, chopped
- olive oil for browning
- 1 oz salt
- ½ oz ground cumin
- 64 oz water

In a stock pot, brown chicken. Transfer chicken to a plate. Add onion to the stock pot and cook until soft. Add salt and garbanzo beans. Add the chicken back to the stock pot and add the cumin and water. Cover and simmer for one hour.

Makes 10–14 servings

Souvlaki

- beef, lamb, pork or chicken
- vegetable or olive oil
- salt and pepper
- oregano
- onions
- bell pepper

Trim the meat as needed and cut meat and vegetables into chunks. Marinate in oil, salt, pepper, and oregano for at least two hours in the fridge. Place meat chunks along with onion and bell pepper on skewers. Broil.

Lamb with Green Peas

- olive oil for browning
- 4 onions, sliced thin
- salt to taste
- 2 tomatoes, chopped
- 12 lamb shanks
- 1 oz (approx) dill
- 7½ lbs green peas (12 oz/ serving)

Salt lamb shanks and brown on all sides until seared. Remove from pan and keep warm. Sauté onions in same pan until onions are just soft. Add tomatoes and sauté for two to three minutes more. Add peas. Sprinkle dill weed over top of lamb shanks and cover with lid or foil. Cook for two and a half to three hours at 325F.

Serves 12

Lamb with Orzo

- 12 lamb shanks
- olive oil for browning lamb
- 1¼ gallon water
- 1–2 cups tomato puree
- 2½ oz salt, approx
- ½ oz black pepper
- 10–12 whole cloves
- 1 whole cinnamon stick, broken into pieces
- ¾ lb butter, approx
- 1½ lbs orzo

Add olive oil to pan. Brown lamb over medium high heat until seared on all sides. Lower heat to medium low and add the water, tomato puree, salt, pepper, cloves and cinnamon. Simmer for half hour.

Transfer ingredients to a large baking dish and place in 325F degree oven. Bake for two to two and a half hours or until meat is tender. Meanwhile, melt butter on stove top pan and add orzo, stirring until orzo is browned. Approximately 30 minutes before lamb is done, add orzo to lamb in oven and stir well. Cover, return to oven and cook another 30 minutes.

Makes 12 servings

Lamb in Red Sauce

- 1 6-lb leg of lamb, cut into large bite-sized pieces
- olive oil for browning
- 48 oz (approx) tomato puree
- 1 oz salt
- 2 gallons hot water
- ½ oz black pepper
- 10–12 cloves
- 1 cinnamon stick, broken into pieces
- 1 oz mint

Add olive oil to pan over medium high heat and brown lamb pieces on all sides. Add hot water, salt, black pepper, cloves, cinnamon stick and mint. Boil for 45 minutes or until sauce is slightly reduced. Cover and place in oven and cook for another 45 minutes. Serve with rice pilaf, spaghetti, Greek fries or fried okra.

Serves 12

Meat Puff Stuffing

- oil for browning
- 4½ lbs onions, minced
- 2 oz salt
- 9 lbs ground beef
- 1 heaping tbsp tomato paste
- pinch black pepper
- pinch paprika
- pinch sweet basil
- 1 box puff pastry

Add oil to pan and brown onions and ground beef; add salt. Add tomato paste, black pepper, paprika and basil and simmer for a few minutes to blend flavors. Skim off fat. Cut puff pastry into seven-inch squares. Brush with egg. Add one large scoop of stuffing to center of pastry and fold into triangle, pinching edges to seal. Continue until all filling is used. Bake in 350F degree oven until golden brown.

Desserts and Breads ————

Revani

- 1¼ lbs sugar
- 2½ lbs cake flour
- ¼ lb ground almonds
- 2 oz baking powder
- 20 eggs, beaten well
- 42 oz milk

- 1 lb butter, melted
- syrup—approx 6–8 ladles, enough to cover Revani pieces
- 4 tbsp vanilla
- 6 tbsp lemon extract

Mix all dry ingredients together and almonds. Add eggs, milk, vanilla, and lemon extract. Stir well. Add butter and mix well until fully incorporated. Spread in pan. Bake at 350F degrees until golden brown. Let cool. Cut into 40 pieces and pour all of the hot syrup over top of cooled Revani, allowing syrup to thoroughly soak in.

Honey Syrup

- 2 gallons hot water
- 20 lbs sugar
- 4 lbs honey
- 3 sticks cinnamon, broken
- 15 whole cloves
- 5 lemons, quartered

Combine all ingredients and boil until it thickens into a syrup. Strain and pour syrup over cooled baked item.

Rice Pudding

- 1 gallon milk
- 1¼ lbs converted rice, rinsed
- 1½ lbs sugar
- 2 tbsp vanilla, to taste

Heat the milk and sugar in a large pan until the milk starts to foam up. Add the rice to the pan and stir until thick. Cook uncovered until rice is tender and milk is absorbed, about 30 minutes.

Makes 14–16 servings

Pastelli

- 64 oz sesame seeds
- 5 lbs honey
- 1 cup walnuts, chopped
- olive oil

Toast the sesame seeds on a flat pan in a 375F degree oven for about 30 minutes until light brown. Set aside. In a large pot, heat honey on high heat until foam appears. Add the sesame seeds, stirring until mixed well and sesame seeds begin to stick to bottom of pot. Add walnuts, stirring well, and cook for about two to three minutes.

Right before mixture begins to burn, remove from heat. Coat a half sheet baking pan with olive oil and spread the mixture evenly onto the sheet. Using the flat side of a turner or spatula, flatten/press the mixture firmly. When cool, cut into 2" × 2" squares, then in half diagonally to make triangles.

Makes 42 pieces

Copenhagen

- 12 cups cake flour
- 5 cups sugar
- 5–6 oz ground cinnamon, to taste
- 2 eggs
- 2 lbs butter
- raspberry jam
- filo dough, partial box
- melted butter for brushing filo

Mix dry ingredients together. Add eggs and mix well. Melt the butter and add to the mixture to make a dough. Spread evenly into a greased 19" × 9 ½" × 1 ½" pan and bake at 350F degrees until light brown and dough is cooked through, about 30 minutes. Remove from oven and cool. Spread the raspberry jam over the top.

Folding four leaves filo dough in half—two the long way and two the short way—lay each of the four leaves half inside the baking sheet and half outside, matching the long/short leaves to the long/short sides of the pan.

Gently spread the mix (below) over the dough and filo leaves. Fold the outside portion of the filo leaves over the mix. Fold another filo sheet in half and lay over the mix to cover the center, as needed. Add four more filo leaves on top and brush with butter.

Score the top into five even scores along the long side. Bake at 350F degrees for approximately 45 minutes. If it's cooked through remove from oven. If it's not quite done put back in oven for a little while longer. Pour hot honey syrup over cooled Copenhagen or cooled syrup over hot Copenhagen. Cut each long slice into eight pieces.

Mix:

- 4 cups chopped almonds
- 3 cups bread crumbs
- 2 cups sugar
- 2 oz baking powder
- 20 eggs
- 3 oz whiskey

Mix nuts, bread crumbs, sugar, baking powder, and eggs. Add whiskey and mix well.

Makes 40 pieces

Pantespani—Sponge Cake

- 45 eggs
- 3 lbs sugar
- 3⅛ lbs cake flour, sifted
- 3½ oz baking powder
- 2 cups water
- 4 oz cocoa (for chocolate Pantespani)

Beat eggs with sugar and water at slow then at medium speed. Add water near end of mixing. Remove from machine and add sifted flour with baking powder. Mix by hand in smooth strokes. Line pans with parchment paper and spread into pan. Bake at 325 to 350F degrees for about 30 minutes.

Cheese Cake

- 1 lb ricotta cheese
- 1 lb cream cheese
- 3 cups sugar
- 4 eggs
- ½ cup starch
- ½ cup flour
- 2 tbsp vanilla
- 4 cups sour cream

Mix together in mixer on low speed the ricotta, cream cheese, and sugar. Turn to high speed and add eggs one at a time. Return to low speed and add remaining ingredients. Spread on half sheet pan and bake on low heat (300F degrees) until set.

Galactoboureko

- 1 gallon milk, divided
- 2½ cups farina flour
- 24 oz sugar, divided
- 14 eggs
- ½ lb filo leaves
- ½ lb butter
- 1 tbsp vanilla
- 1 tbsp lemon extract

Custard: In a medium saucepan bring to boil 10 cups of the milk with 14 oz of the sugar. In a separate large pan, mix eggs, remaining sugar and milk, and flour by hand. When milk boils, pour contents of bowl into other pan gradually and stir until thick. Add vanilla and lemon extract.

Baking pan: Butter the pan. Place filo two layers per side, half in, half out. Brush with butter. Add two more sheets, half in and half out, brush with butter. Fill with custard mix, fold leaves toward center and brush with butter. Add four more filo sheets on top. Brush with butter and score eight cuts along the long side. Bake at 350F degrees until cooked through. Cut five rows along the short side.

Makes 40 pieces

Honey Bars

- 1½ lbs sugar
- 12 oz shortening
- 2 oz baking soda
- 20 eggs
- ½ lb honey
- 1 lb raisins
- 2 lbs cake flour
- 5 lbs bread flour
- 3 tbsp cinnamon

Mix all ingredients together on low speed for two to three minutes. Add eggs and mix on medium low speed for about 10 minutes. Divide mixture into eight pieces and shape into logs. Place onto half sheet pan lined with parchment paper; flatten. Bake at 350F degrees for 40–60 minutes. Remove from oven and cut each log into eight pieces. Brush with honey syrup.

Tsoureki—Greek Easter Bread

- 32 oz warm water
- 5 oz yeast
- 1½ lbs bread flour

Dissolve yeast in warm water. Add bread flour and mix well. Add the rest of the ingredients, below, and mix thoroughly in machine. Cover and let rise. Stir down in machine. Remove dough and divide/shape into loaves as desired. Bake at 350F degrees until done, about 30 minutes.

- 5 lbs bread flour
- 28 oz shortening
- 28 oz sugar
- 1½ oz ground mahlepi
- 3–4 orange peels, grated
- 20 eggs

Kourabiethes

- 8 oz butter
- 2 lbs shortening
- 12 oz sugar
- 1 orange peel, grated
- 1 oz vanilla
- 10 lbs cake flour
- 3 lbs ground almonds
- Spray of rose water

Mix all ingredients together and cut with ice cream scoop to be even and place in a parchment lined full sheet baking pan. Bake at 325F degrees for one to one and a half hours or until barely browned.

Coconut Macaroons

- 1 lb egg whites
- 2 lbs sugar
- 2 oz honey
- 1¾ lbs shredded coconut

Preheat oven to 350F degrees. Combine all ingredients in a bowl. Chill. Spoon onto a nonstick or greased cookie sheet. Bake in the oven for one and a half to two hours until lightly browned.

Butter Cookies

- 1½ lbs sugar
- 1½ lbs shortening
- 10 lbs butter
- 10 eggs
- 5 oz vanilla
- 1½ lbs pastry flour
- 1 oz baking powder
- 1½ lbs cake flour

Preheat oven to 350F. Beat the sugar, shortening, butter, eggs, and vanilla on low speed to combine then medium/high speed to mix. Add the dry ingredients slowly until thoroughly combined. Use a pastry cone to squeeze out cookies onto a non-stick or greased cookie sheet. Bake in the oven for one hour or until tops are browned.

Sugar Cookies

- 1½ lbs sugar
- 9 oz shortening
- 1 lb butter
- 5 eggs
- 1 tsp nutmeg
- ¼ oz vanilla
- ¼ oz almond extract
- ¼ oz baking soda
- 3¾ lbs cake flour

Mix all ingredients together in mixer on slow speed. Place mixture in a pastry bag. Extrude cookies onto a cookie sheet lined with parchment paper. Bake until nicely browned.

Almond Cookies

- 7 lbs almond paste
- 7½ lbs powdered sugar
- 3½ lbs ground almonds
- 3½ lbs egg whites
- vanilla and lemon extracts, to taste

Mix all together in mixer on slow speed. Put mixture in a pastry bag.

Extrude cookies onto a cookie sheet lined with pastry paper. Bake 350 degrees for one to one and a half hours.

Chocolate Chip Cookies (with nuts)

- 1 lb brown sugar
- 8 oz shortening
- 8 eggs
- 1 tsp baking soda
- 1½ oz vanilla

- 16 oz nuts
- 2 lbs cake flour
- 12 oz chocolate chips
- 1 tsp ground cloves

Preheat oven to 350F degrees. Combine all ingredients in a bowl. Chill. Spoon onto a nonstick or greased cookie sheet. Bake for six to ten minutes.

Chapter Notes

Introduction

1. Dan Georgakas, "Greek-American Radicalism: The Twentieth Century," *Journal of the Hellenic Diaspora* 20 (1994): 9. Italics in the original.

2. Georgakas, "Radicalism," 7.

3. Deborah Lupton cited in Krishnendu Ray, *The Ethnic Restaurateur* (London: Bloomsbury, 2016), xiii.

4. Edward J. Erler, Thomas G. West, and John Marini, *The Founders on Citizenship and Immigration: Principles and Challenges in America* (Lanham, MD: Rowman & Littlefield, 2007), 108.

5. Matthew Frye Jacobson, *Whiteness of a Different Color: European Immigrants and the Alchemy of Race* (Cambridge: Harvard University Press, 1999) and Yiorgos Anagnostou, *The Contours of White Ethnicity: Popular Ethnography and the Making of Usable Past in Greek America* (Athens: Ohio University Press, 2009).

6. Krishnendu Ray, *The Ethnic Restaurateur* (London: Bloomsbury, 2016), 116.

7. Ted Merwin, *Pastrami on Rye: An Overstuffed History of the Jewish Deli* (New York: New York University Press, 2015), 3.

8. Merwin, *Pastrami*, 3.

9. Merwin, *Pastrami*, 3.

10. Merwin, *Pastrami*, 2.

11. Shachar M. Pinsker, *A Rich Brew: How Cafes Created Modern Jewish Culture* (New York: New York University Press, 2018), 12.

12. Merwin, *Pastrami*, 7.

13. Jennifer 8. Lee, *The Fortune Cookie Chronicles: Adventures in the World of Chinese Food* (New York: Twelve, 2008), 19.

14. Lee, *Fortune Cookie*, 19.

15. Lee, *Fortune Cookie*, 26.

16. Pinsker, *Rich Brew*, 9.

17. Lily Cho, *Eating Chinese: Culture on the Menu in Small Town Canada* (Toronto: University of Toronto Press, 2010), 7.

18. For a good starting point about feminist labor, please see Gayatri Chakravorty Spivak, "Diasporas Old and New: Women in the Transnational World," *Textual Practice* 10:2 (1996): 245–69.

Chapter One

1. Krishnendu Ray, *The Ethnic Restaurateur* (London: Bloomsbury, 2016), 72.

Chapter Two

1. Quote from Kenneth Clark, *Civilisation*, BBC-TV Series, 1969, Episode 13, 33:05.

2. Gergely Baics, *Feeding Gotham: The Political Economy and Geography of Food in New York City, 1790–1860* (Princeton: Princeton University Press).

3. Calculation from *www.dollartimes.com*.

4. Taso G. Lagos, *American Zeus: The Unique Life and Tragic Trials of Alexander Pantages, Theater Mogul* (Jefferson, NC: McFarland, 2017).

Chapter Three

1. As I write this, it is presently a "State Social House" restaurant.

2. From *http://la.eater.com/2013/5/*

169

13/6435783/the-source-las-first-spiritual
-vegetarian-restaurant.

3. From *http://la.eater.com/2013/5/
13/6435783/the-source-las-first-spiritual
-vegetarian-restaurant.*

Chapter Four

1. Much of this history of the University District that follows comes from Wikipedia—https://en.wikipedia.org/wiki/University_District,_Seattle—as well as my own knowledge gleaned in conversations with locals over the years.

Chapter Seven

1. Anthony Flint, *Wrestling with Moses: How Jane Jacobs Took On New York's Master Builder and Transformed the American City* (New York: Random House, 2011).

2. Albert Lee, *Call Me Roger* (Chicago: Contemporary Books, 1988).

Chapter Ten

1. Michael Levine, director, *Streit's: Matzo and the American Dream* (Unleavened Bread LLC, 2016).

2. Elissa Sampson, interviewee, *Streit's*, 2016.

3. Sampson, *Streit's*, 2016.

4. Sampson, *Streit's*, 2016.

5. Sampson, *Streit's*, 2016.

Conclusion

1. Ray, *Ethnic Restaurateur*, 19, 63–110.

Index

Numbers in *bold italics* indicate pages with illustrations

171

Index

Index

Index

Index

Index